W9-CUI-035

Trojan Peace:
Some Deterrence Propositions Tested

Theresa C. Smith

MONOGRAPH SERIES
IN WORLD AFFAIRS

Graduate School of International Studies

UNIVERSITY OF DENVER

VOLUME NINETEEN

Book One
RESEARCH GAPS IN ALLIANCE DYNAMICS
Michael Don Ward

Book Two
TROJAN PEACE:
SOME DETERRENCE PROPOSITIONS TESTED
Theresa C. Smith

Book Three
THE CONSISTENCY, SOUNDNESS AND APPLICABILITY
OF THE BALANCE OF POWER THEORY
Roslyn Simowitz

Book Four
INTERNATIONAL POLICY COORDINATION:
A GAME THEORETIC STUDY OF
ISSUES AND NECESSARY CONDITIONS
Martin W. Sampson III

MONOGRAPH SERIES IN WORLD AFFAIRS

Graduate School of International Studies
University of Denver
Denver, Colorado 80208

Editor . . . . Karen A. Feste
Managing Editor . . . . Millie Van Wyke

Editorial Board

William Bader
U.S. Senate

Steven Brams
New York University

James Caporaso
University of Denver

Jerome Clubb
University of Michigan

Catherine Kelleher
University of Denver

Robert Jervis
University of California-
   Los Angeles

Michael O'Leary
Syracuse University

Todd Sandler
University of Wyoming

Susan Strange
London School of Economics
   and Political Science

Kenneth Thompson
University of Virginia

John Turner
University of Minnesota

Dina Zinnes
University of Illinois

TROJAN PEACE:
SOME DETERRENCE PROPOSITIONS TESTED

Theresa C. Smith

Volume 19
Book 2

MONOGRAPH SERIES IN WORLD AFFAIRS

Graduate School of International Studies
University of Denver
Denver, Colorado 80208

WITHDRAWN 972

COLORADO COLLEGE LIBRARY
COLORADO SPRINGS,
COLORADO

Library of Congress Cataloging in Publication Data

Smith, Theresa C., 1951-
 Trojan peace.

 (Monograph series in world affairs, ISSN 0077-0582; v. 19, bk. 2)
 Bibliography: p.
 1. Deterrence (Strategy) I. Title. II. Series.
U162.6.S53   1982   355'.0217   82-11771
ISBN 0-87940-069-2

© University of Denver (Colorado Seminary) 1982
  Printed in The United States of America

355.0217
Sm67t

ABOUT THE AUTHOR

T. C. SMITH is an Assistant Professor of Political Science at Rutgers University. She is currently analyzing some domestic pressure factors in the American defense budget. Her other ongoing research examines the recent failure of the chemical weapons negotiations. Professor Smith is also collaborating with Professor Thomas A. Oleszczuk to compile a data bank on Soviet repression of dissent. Smith's "Arms Race Instability and War," testing for a relation between constrained mathematical stability characteristics and political outcome of arms races, appeared in *Journal of Conflict Resolution,* June 1980.

ACKNOWLEDGEMENTS

The author appreciates the thoughtful contributions of the reviewers and the technical assistance of Mabel Jin-min Hsueh. This research was funded by the Rutgers University Research Council Grant Program.

. . . From discussions with policymakers in the Pentagon, it is clear that there has been no adequate exploration of the nature of deterrence.

—A. Waskov, 1962

TABLE OF CONTENTS

Trojan Peace:
Some Deterrence Propositions Tested

INTRODUCTION

An extensive literature on deterrence theory appeared in the West after World War II and, perhaps to a lesser extent, in the USSR after Stalin. (See among the many major works Snyder, 1961; Quester, 1966; Green, 1966; Kintner, 1967; George and Smoke, 1974; Sokolovsky, 1975.) This literature is essentially hypothetical, and while its propositions are often argued in generally applicable abstract terms, it appears to be drawn largely from one dyadic case, the Soviet-American cold war. In the developing world, a new deterrence literature largely divorced from superpower doctrine has begun to appear sporadically over the last two decades, evidently as a precursor of nuclear proliferation. While avoiding some of the superpower idiosyncracies, this literature is also largely case-specific, and historical.

The bulk of the deterrence literature cited in the West is U.S.-NATO in origin and bipolar in conceptualization. There is no reason to expect doctrines arising in other places to share the central ideas, number of players or historical lines of development which characterize the North Atlantic thinking, although the para bellum hypothesis is widely heard. Indigenous lines of argument will arise, as K. Subrahmanyam, Director of India's Institute for Defense Studies and Analyses, has abruptly exclaimed:

> The absurd doctrines of the 50's and 60's, propounded by the Western military-industrial-intellectual complex to justify an aggressive arms race, are also repeated by many of the proponents of the weapons program in India. This, of course, is to be expected. When a Western intellectual asks an Indian what is his doctrine for justifying a weapons program, it very rarely occurs to the former that the various doctrines, the counterforce and countervalue strikes, the mutual assured destruction, graduated escalation, the first strike doctrine in Europe, etc., may sound as stupid to Indians as the Dullesian doctrine of rolling back international Communism or Dean Rusk's perception about a billion Chinese armed with nuclear weapons (Kemp, et al., 1974:129).

3

The deterrence literature in general would then be enriched by the addition of empirical studies which test some of the fundamental presumptions of various deterrence arguments in as extensive and varied an international data base as can be constructed.

Some quantitative work already addresses the para bellum question directly (Naroll, 1964, 1969; and Naroll, Bullough and Naroll, 1974). In a more recent study, Wallace (1981) compares the war-predicting capacity of an index of arms racing against the performance of some possible deterrent predictors. The present analysis examines the results of some discriminant functions using force ratios as arguably successful deterrents over the course of twenty-eight international arms competitions since 1877.

DETERRENCE THEORIZING

Deterrence theory has been given numerous rigorous quantitative and nonquantitative analyses (Aron, 1959; Ellsberg, 1960, 1961, 1968; Snyder, 1961; Garthoff, 1962; Green, 1966; Quester, 1966; George and Smoke, 1974; among others). Snyder (1961) implies that deterrence succeeds when the product of one country's threat times the perceived probability of acting on the threat (credibility) exceeds the product of the value to a rival of a given objective times the presumed probability of obtaining the objective via military means. Obviously, despite the appeal of this kind of schema, many of these quantities can be given only the crudest and most judgmental approximate values. It is unclear that such subjective probabilities satisfy the axioms of the probability calculus. Further, the calculation itself, and others like it, have been well criticized and can be shown to fail under several circumstances, as when threats or objectives are assigned infinite values (Cantor, 1955; Deutsch, 1968).

Because measures of values of objectives are inaccessible and because psychological and geopolitical factors (such as knowing other decision makers' intentions or their perceived strategic evaluation of Patagonia) impinge on the calculations, the workings of deterrence tend to be debated, for purposes of policy as well as occasionally for theoretical reasons, via comparisons of force ratios between adversaries. The apparently more accurate but elusive considerations of importance of particular objectives and the probability of achieving such objectives by military means are set aside. This simpler tack—studying unadorned force comparisons—is taken here for the purpose of extracting some testable assertions on the prevalence of certain force ratios in periods of peacetime competition between rivals.

This does not mean that there is general agreement on what force levels actually obtain in any particular rivalry, what the relevant comparisons are, or how they should be interpreted. Fundamental differences in approach to capabilities/threat assessment continue to exist, so that even works published in the same year can show great disparity or even overt contradiction

5

on such basic questions as the significance of the relative force standings of the superpowers. Compare Booth, Teller and Speed:

> . . . the typical U.S. strategist would argue . . . The strategic balance should never be allowed to become delicate, for bears are too unruly (Booth, 1979:41).

> If Soviet leaders had not responded to a less confrontational and threatening military strategy, then little would have been lost: there was always enough overkill to ensure that deterrence was not "delicate": Politically speaking, the balance of terror was never delicate: the error in thinking it was, was the result of an imbalance in the outlook of worst-case advocates (Booth, 1979:125).

> But the balance, which unfortunately is a balance of terror, is once again threatening to become delicate (Teller in Speed, 1979:Foreword).

> . . . It has not been fully recognized that the world is now entering a period in which the "balance of terror" is once again becoming delicate (Speed, 1979:15).

Speed and Teller's view contrasts markedly with that of McIntyre and Kissinger a few years earlier, and recalls the famous Wohlstetter (1959) article on the delicate balance of terror:

> I think there is common agreement that at no time in the post-war period has the Soviet Union had a strategic superiority over the United States in any significant category (Kissinger, U.S. Senate Committee on Foreign Relations, 1974:Y4.S76/2; D/48;2:260).

> The preoccupation with the research and development arms race has obscured how thoroughly secure the strategic balance is now and for the practical future. My Subcommittee has probed into every possible Soviet degradation of our strategic force and has been assured in detail from [former] Secretary Schlesinger, to the most talented program specialist, that there can be no doubt whatever that our deterrent is secure; that our second strike capability is secure; that our ability to respond flexibly against large numbers and a wide variety of Soviet military targets is secure (McIntyre, 1975).

Precisely because there is little consensus on subjective factors affecting force comparisons, there is a need for a measure of forces which is as objective as possible. Here military budget data are used, since these are a standard approximation for capabilities (Abolfathi, 1975) and may in any case tap intentions to some variable degree because intentions and capabilities are interdependent (Freedman, 1977:10-11).

Following the assumption that deterrence may be studied via comparisons of rival forces, the second assumption made for the purposes of this analysis is that deterrence is a general and not time-bound phenomenon.

That is, the calculations are purported to hold over time, across cultures, and across generations of weaponry, and are not unique or specific to the post-1945 period. Many writers note that the advent of nuclear explosives did not inspire the creation of new deterrence arguments, but merely clarified pre-Hiroshima views (Quester, 1966). In this vein Speed comments:

> The concept of deterrence was not born with the nuclear age; it has long been a part of international politics. Countries have always tried to induce fear in an adversary or at least to create strong doubts about the outcome of any possible aggression . . . The introduction of nuclear weapons potentially changed this situation because it simplified the calculations (Speed, 1979:7).

Similarly, Jervis observes:

> . . . although deterrence does not require nuclear weapons, their existence makes it easier to grasp the basic ideas (Jervis, 1979:290).

If they are correct, deterrence is not time-bound. This assertion is supported by reports of the ancient historians on the political use of implied threat via standing capabilities (Xenophon, 1949:82).

Writers drawing on Gallois' proportional deterrence school also cross the conventional/nuclear divide in their arguments, holding that deterrence operates at levels beneath superpower rivalries and can be used to restrain an aggressor operating with only conventional weapons. If this is so, deterrence operates among vastly unequal adversaries, and across generations of weapons (Lefever, 1979:8).

Cross-cultural force comparisons seem at least in principle to pose some difficulties for international testing of deterrence propositions, since there exist national variations in the structure of arguments about deterrence, hence in doctrine and in applied policy. These differences are based on national historical experience, ideology, practical necessity (Mao's pre-1964 "paper tiger," after which the Chinese acquired their own paper tiger), and underlying special strengths and vulnerabilities of the countries in question. This complexity is reflected in differing emphases within the armed forces, as well as in the degree of vogue in which civil defense and other defense vs. deterrence questions find themselves; and it yields somewhat different configurations of conventional and nuclear forces across countries. Thus care must be exercised when comparing military forces across nations, since forces serve a congeries of domestic as well as foreign functions to some degree (Schilling, Hammond and Snyder, 1962).

None of this implies that the question of relative superiority cannot be given a reasonable answer, even though doctrine and force configurations do follow national idiosyncracies. Probably the most accurate answers can only be given on a case-by-case basis by area military experts. However, the question of relative superiority of forces arises cross-culturally and is given some fairly definite answers in military planning—though these be crude. Consider British authorizations in 1909 to outbuild Germany, in Dreadnoughts, by a fixed ratio of 8/4 (Albertini, 1928, 1:323). There is also the program in China in the 1860s to produce a standing army and an arsenal "unsurpassed" in the West (Wright, 1957:196-220). Hence for some purposes a summary measure of forces actually is used, and is probably appropriate for an internationally based study of this kind. The cultural difficulties these comparisons may encounter are mitigated by the observed tendency of rivals to compete in the same or highly similar vehicles and munitions manufactured in the same countries (Peru and Chile in the late 1800s) or duplicated domestically.

Accordingly, the assumption that deterrence is a general and not time-bound process is not a novel assumption in the literature (Legault and Lindsey, 1974:140), but it has seldom been applied empirically. Neither is the view (incorporated here) that the perspective of the challenger country deserves study a novel one. Jervis writes, "Most of the (Western?) literature is written from the standpoint of the country resisting change, but the principles are more general . . ." (Jervis, 1979:297).

However, there seems to be some disagreement over these general principles as they relate to war and peace. Many Western analysts contend that the superiority of a status quo power preserves peace and, conversely, that revisionist superiority is dangerous. Other Western writers concerned with the overkill question and with arms control believe that superiority and its consequent perceived inequalities cause war while parity is most likely to produce peace, ceteris paribus. But researchers who hold that some nations are inherently aggressive are inclined to argue that parity is perilous when aggressive nations are involved, since an aggressive rival who is not in a demonstrably inferior position may feel an incentive to attack. Then, when the rivals believed to be aggressive are identified as they are in Soviet, Chinese and other non-Western accounts, superior forces for the challenger state deter status quo countries from inciting wars. These basic propositions are elaborated below:

Proposition 1: Status quo superiority makes for peace, revisionist superiority for war

Throughout a large part of the writing on deterrence, the most basic proposition appears to be that clear superiority in the hands of the right power preserves the peace, while superiority in the wrong hands is intrinsically risky, even if it is not actively used. This proposition has been expressed in a variety of terms, generally neglecting the possibility that superiority could be used by a "right-minded" (i.e., status quo) power for a predatory or other war; or as political muscle in an incident which might induce war, such as the rumored U.S. nuclear threat against North Korea in 1975. Statements supporting the proposition that status quo superiority augurs for peace while revisionist superiority promotes a war risk include, inter alia:

> . . . [In the last fifteen years, the U.S. vis-a-vis the USSR] we have sunk from superiority to inferiority in strategic nuclear capabilities . . . Either we restore our [formerly superior] nuclear armed might so as to deter nuclear war or we go on playing catch-up . . . with no hope of reaching parity [even in conventional weapons] (Beilenson and Cohen, 1982:36).

> . . . The only conceivable way to deter the Russians from exploiting their military advantages in regions such as the Persian Gulf is by confronting them with superior theater nuclear forces (see Russett, 1963) . . . To prevent nuclear war, the U.S. should augment its nuclear armory . . . with an ample margin of safety (Beilenson and Cohen, 1982:44).

> Not only has the Soviet approach [to deterrence] been dismissed as primitive . . . their programmes have been seen to be so misconceived that . . . their weapons deployment has threatened to undermine the stability of the balance of terror. Against such an adversary, it has been argued, overinsurance is the only rational policy (Booth, 1979:42).

> The comprehensive nature of the growing Soviet threat requires a comparably comprehensive NATO response in order to sustain NATO's deterrent strategy and so maintain a stable peace (Burt, 1981:3).

(While Burt's statement may be an argument for equal increments, or for parity, or for preservation of a current imbalance by adding proportional amounts to each side, it appears in context to be the latter, favoring NATO forces.)

> . . . as much official American opinion holds . . . Soviet acquisition of superior strategic forces would presumably encourage still more bellicose behavior . . . [i.e., more bellicose than attacks on U.S. allies] (Coffey, 1971:37).

> There are two ways of looking at the question of how much deterrence is enough. One is to examine the relative military power of Russia with the thought that the best deterrence is to maintain superior power. That has been the dominant United States view for the last thirty years. It has always been politically popular to say that "we must be number one" (Cox, A., 1976:208).

> . . . if a serious deterrent gap ever occurred, then, even if the Soviets were not willing, either out of caution or morality, to use their superiority, the situation would still be dangerous (Kahn, 1960:759).

Under these circumstances [Soviet strategic advantage] the U.S. might refuse Soviet demands and threaten to fight; yet the strategic inferiority of the U.S. might lead the Soviets to misinterpret these threats as bluff. The result could be the very war that the unilateralists [unilateral disarmers] as well as the author, wish to avoid (Kintner, 1967:241).

They [the Communist-controlled states] have chosen (peaceful) coexistence because unless they achieve decisive superiority, the destruction wrought by nuclear arms would be entirely disproportionate to the goals they are committed to pursue. The contrary might prove to be the case if they do achieve superiority (Kintner, 1967: 283).

So long as we maintain a superior general-war capability, so long as we maintain a clearly definable deterrent margin, all forms of Soviet military and political aggression [and consequent war] will be inhibited (Hahn and Neff, 1960:190).

We are not going to permit the Soviets to outdistance us, because to do so would be to jeopardize our very viability as a nation (McNamara, 1968:61).

. . . What has kept the peace . . . has been the immense [U.S. strategic] superiority . . . (Nixon, New York Times, 30 October 1968:29).

Actually, the reason why there has been no general nuclear war so far is a very simple one—we have not been merely as strong as or a little stronger than the Soviets; we have had overwhelming military superiority. Although the Soviets have managed to whittle down what I call our "deterrent margin"—the scope and degree of our military superiority—I am confident that we can maintain that deterrent margin large enough to prevent general nuclear war indefinitely and on our terms (Power, 1964:126).

As long as the U.S. can maintain . . . "unpredictability," and . . . some measurable edge of U.S. superiority remains and can clearly be perceived, . . . it may inhibit direct Soviet participation in attacks on America's friends and allies (Kemp, 1974: 19-20).

. . . [because of manpower, conventional forces and geographical "advantages" over the U.S.] . . . even strategic "parity" [not to speak of a Soviet quantitative strategic edge] creates an overall imbalance in favor of the Soviet Union (Kemp, 1974:22-23).

(The argument here and passim in Ra'anan (in Kemp, 1974) is that visible U.S. strategic superiority restrains the "offensive-minded" Kremlin groups from attacks on the U.S. or intervention against U.S. allies or friends.)

. . . to insure America's national security . . . I have repeatedly pledged to halt the decline in America's military strength and restore that margin of safety needed for the protection of the

American people and the maintenance of peace (Reagan, 1981:67).

> . . . if one side could muster a wide margin of forces over its minimum deterrent, while the other side just barely met this criterion, stability would be fairly high if the stronger country were a status quo power with little incentive to strike first. But stability would depend on the continuance of benevolent intentions on the part of the stronger side (Snyder, 1956:98-99).

> There is first what might be called necessary detente, the absolute need for the two powers to evolve techniques for avoiding not only a nuclear conflict but also those international situations which might lead to one. Up to 1955-56 the vast preponderance of America's power offered a reasonable guarantee against such a conflict (Ulam, U.S. Senate Committee on Foreign Relations, 1974:Y4.S76/2;D48;2:115).

> Soviet ideology and nationalistic doctrines have always demanded that the greatest caution be exercised – neither the revolution nor the state must be risked on adventurist policies. Any Soviet attack on the West would undoubtedly be backed by overwhelming military superiority and be aimed at a quick victory (Speed, 1979:114).

> . . . the most dangerous occurrence is not a runaway arms race but the status quo powers losing the arms race (Weede, 1980:286-87).

> The fundamental goal of our defense effort, as I have said, is to preserve peace with freedom. . . . The Soviet buildup . . . is not the only changed threat we must address . . . we have let our strategic superiority be eroded [which is a threat to peace . . .] (Weinberger, 1981:46).

Several Soviet sources could also be cited to the same effect, substituting the Soviet Union for the U.S. as the right-minded power. However, for the sake of the argument presented here, the USSR will be considered as a revisionist power vis-a-vis the U.S., and some Soviet arguments will be noted below.

The literature also includes several assertions which in context support the para bellum proposition, though this support is less explicit in a brief quote:

> Those who scoff at it [the U.S. deterrent] ignore the plain fact that the deterrent has preserved the peace. The only thing that can tame Communist fanaticism, Russian or Chinese, is fear of failure, and the deterrent has kept that salutary fear alive (Kintner, 1967:44).

> A policy of deterrence assumes that . . . any relaxation of military preparedness will endanger the security of the U.S. (Lyons and Morton, 1965:17).

11

. . . high quality deterrence, not unilateral restraint to the point of eroding deterrence, is the surest way of avoiding nuclear war (Nitze, 1976:211).

. . . to minimize the risks of nuclear war, it would seem to me wise to assure that no enemy could believe he could profit from a war (Nitze, 1976:232).

Proposition 2: Parity promotes peace: inequalities risk war

Perhaps the second most basic proposition in the deterrence literature, and one which poses immediate inconsistencies with the first, is that superiority on *either* side risks war, while rough equality promotes peace. (For a further application of this view in the context of reducing pressures for a preemptive nuclear attack during implementation of arms control, see Kissinger, 1960.) Several authors, military officers, academics and others contribute directly to this para parity literature:

> The Soviets believe that as a consequence of the arrival of strategic parity, the United States and the West were forced to accept detente, or peaceful coexistence [as opposed to overt violence] . . . as a general guideline for capitalism's interactions with socialism (Gilbert, 1977:47).

> Another possibility for preventive war could occur if [an arms control agreement broke down and] one side had a considerable lead . . . [but not if rough parity obtained] (Kahn, 1960:759).

> We cannot allow the Soviets unilaterally to obtain a counterforce option that we ourselves lack. We must have a symmetrical balancing of the strategic forces on both sides (Cox, 1976:86).

> . . . the lack of equality can become a source of serious diplomatic and military miscalculation. Opponents may feel that they can exploit a favorable imbalance by means of political pressure, as Hitler did so skillfully in the 1930's, particularly with Neville Chamberlain at Berchtesgaden (Schlesinger, Time, 11 February 1974:20).

(Schlesinger's statement appears, perhaps erroneously, to be a parity argument.)

> At the level of conceptualization there has been a lingering assumption in many quarters that our security is best served by seeking to maintain clear superiority over the Soviet Union . . . It has not yet come to terms with the fact that nuclear superiority in any practically significant sense cannot be achieved by either side, and that the quest for superiority can only result in a further decline in real security for both sides. A more reasonable approach would seem to be . . . a military equilibrium—necessarily, an asymmetrical balance—at as stable and moderate a level as can be managed by negotiation (Shulman, U.S. Senate Committee on Foreign Relations, 1974:Y4.S76/2;D/48;2:106).

Without parity there cannot be negotiations but without negotiations there cannot be peace (Spadolini, New York Times,
13 September 1981:20).

Proposition 3: Equality promotes war when one side is a challenger

A third basic proposition in the Western deterrence literature is that
equality between adversaries promotes the risk of war, especially when one
rival is "revisionist." We might expect to see this proposition borne out
where the revisionist power perceives itself at a turning point (local maximum) in its arming, anticipating a military decline and continued foreign
confrontation. Rough equality would then provide the revisionist power its
best anticipatable force ratio, hence its optimal moment to attack, ceteris
paribus (Voevodsky, 1969, 1970, 1972; Alcock, 1972; Alcock and Young,
1973; Wallace and Wilson, 1978; and other writers on the periodicity of
arming patterns). The view that military equality is dangerous, especially
between countries of unequal status, is espoused by Kaysen, Coffey, and
Pfister among others:

> . . . as much official American opinion holds . . . the achieve-
> ment by the USSR of strategic parity, however defined, could
> "liberate" forms of conflict that had been precluded previously,
> including "even military action, against allies of the United
> States . . ." (Coffey, 1971:37). (See also Horelick and Rush,
> 1965:166-67.)
>
> . . . any claim to (military) equality by the morally and eco-
> nomically inferior Soviet Union is at best presumptuous, at
> worst dangerous (Kaysen, 1968:675).

This argument has partial similarities to those advanced by international
relations researchers investigating status inconsistency and war, though the
implications may be at variance. In crude summary this literature argues
that inequities between ascribed and achieved status, mediated by formal
alliance and international organization membership, are consistent war
predictors, and that changes in armed forces may be important producers of
status inconsistency.

In Wallace (1971), rates of weapons growth had a direct effect on war,
and status inconsistency was highly and significantly associated with war.
While Wallace shows arms racing itself to be war related, his analysis also
underlines the potential deterrence failure risk created between rivals who
compete in equal capabilities and unequal ascribed status. Rough parity, or
a situation approaching parity, with only minor differences in force levels,
may then be associated with deterrence failure especially following periods
of major inequalities in arms (yielding status inconsistency) or times of
contention in foreign policy.

Pfister (1974:61) writes: ". . . mistrust and even status create a compulsion to war." In this context also note Kintner's observation (1967) that weapons parity usually augurs for peace, but does not *guarantee* peace if there exist substantial psychological or other differences which confer a putative advantage on one contender. The Singer, Bremer and Stuckey (1972) assumptions are also relevant here. If parity increases uncertainty (especially with regard to the identity of the probable victor in any confrontation) and if uncertainty *reduces* reluctance to fight (this may be argued both ways), rough parity will be tied to deterrence failure. Alexandroff and Rosecrance (1977) see World War II as such a case of deterrence failure by parity, as well as by miscalculation of time horizons, with Germany focused on short-term advantage and the United Kingdom expecting to succeed in the long term.

Proposition 4: Superiority of the challenger state safeguards peace; status quo superiority risks war

The "status quo-revisionist" distinctions as used by American and West European analysts are not easily applied to the rest of the planet, whether Marxist or not, especially since the choice of historical benchmarks used to determine who advocates change—and change away from what—is strongly biased by nationality. The status quo determination is further complicated by the escalation of animosities which characterizes arms racing, since a series of hostile incidents can confuse underlying issues and interests (as per Jervis' treatment of the spiral model, 1976). If we consider socialist countries to be revisionists, this proposition has several Soviet, Chinese and other advocates who believe that it is the superior threat of the socialist forces which forestalls war. Some characteristic assessments include:

> The deepening of the general crisis of capitalism, the aggravation of its contradictions, has led to a still greater intensification of the adventurism and aggressiveness of imperialism. The imperialists so far have not managed to push the world into the hell of thermonuclear war because there exists on our planet such a powerful force as the Soviet Union and its Armed Forces and the armies of other socialist countries (Kintner and Scott, 1967:353-54).

> . . . [the West will continue] achieving military supremacy, undermining the foundations of peace, and at a favorable moment, resolving the international dispute between capitalism and socialism by military means (Brezhnev, in Krasnaya Zvezda, 28 March 1973).

> . . . a class analysis must be made. Whether or not nuclear weapons help peace depends on who possesses them. It is detrimental to peace if they are in the hands of imperialist countries; it helps peace if they are in the hands of socialist countries (Peking Review, 16 August 1963:12).

In the socialist states, on the contrary, the strengthening of their armed forces serves as a sort of counterweight to the capitalist armies, creates a reliable guarantee for the preservation of peace and increases the chances of preventing war (Sokolovsky, 1975:225).

. . . political and economic potentialities are being created to prevent a world war, even though imperialism still remains . . . These potentialities are determined, first and foremost, by the great military power of the socialist camp, which is now an insuperable obstacle in the pathway to the unleashing of a new world war by the imperialist madmen (Sokolovsky, 1975:384).

While Sokolovsky does not speak overtly of superiority here, this view will be understood to mean that superiority for "revisionist" countries' forces works for peace. This contention has been argued in the USSR and elsewhere, and some Western scholars have suggested that Soviet superiority might not necessarily be disastrous for U.S. interests:

. . . because of the uncertainties . . . and risks . . . it does not follow that shifts in the strategic balance will necessarily nerve the USSR to run greater risks . . . or . . . to adopt more bellicose, expansionist foreign policies . . . not . . . even superior strategic forces would enable the USSR to win every showdown by default (Coffey, 1971:38).

Obviously the socialist countries can only prevent war if war is not a foreordained part of this stage of human social development. This view was handily elaborated by Khrushchev who, in the post-Stalin reforms, argued vigorously that war was not "fatalistically" inevitable, only possible; and that war was preventable by the Soviet bloc (*Current Digest of the Soviet Press*, 1956:8, 4, 3-15; see also Khrushchev's speech to the Twentieth Party Congress). This development was crucial to detente in that it implied capitalist countries could possibly negotiate sincere arms control (Marantz, 1975). It is interesting to note that the U.S. has recently revived the "inevitability of [superpower] war" doctrine. Sallagar writes:

We must therefore expect that, sooner or later, some act by the Soviet Union or her partners [sic], is likely to create a situation in which the U.S. feels compelled to intervene militarily . . . There is no indication that the possible consequences have been adequately explored . . . (Sallagar, 1980:27).

Walters raises a similar point:

The official view in the West is that the West might be obliged to use nuclear arms first (Walters, 1974:61).

Walters' point is underscored by the lack of interest in "no first use" agreements, and by the recent declarations in the USSR of a "launch under [surmised] attack" policy complementing the U.S. "launch on warning" policy (Douglass, 1980:62).

15

For further consideration of the apparent convergence between U.S. and Soviet statements on feasibility of nuclear war fighting, or at least on the necessity of preparing to fight such a war, regardless of its feasibility, with some novel notions of the functioning of deterrence within wars, consult U.S. Department of State *Bulletin* 1974:1921; *Foreign Policy* 39, Summer 1980; and *U.S. Presidential Directive* 59, July 1980. While some attempt had been made in the U.S. to accustom troops to the idea of fighting a nuclear war via the U.S. Army Operation Smoky tests in the 1950s and other such programs, the arrival of nuclear war fighting discussion in public foreign policy executive level talks appears to be a recent development.

Proposition 5: Force ratios are not a major determinant of war or peace

There is a growing body of literature which holds that the major factors influencing decisions to go to war have relatively little to do with prevalent force ratios, and considerably more to do with either the factors on the other side of Snyder's deterrence inequality (that is, with the value of the political objective and a [time-constrained] estimate of the probability of attaining the objective); or, with the absolute levels of arming already reached, beyond which differences have no political or military significance. Some writers suggest that after overkill, all (strategic) force ratios represent parity; others, that asymmetries in forces are still militarily meaningful but do not have any necessary political consequences. On these points:

> Superpower deterrence is inherently stable . . . (Baylis and Segal, 1981:91).

> . . . nuclear weapons in the hands of an adversary are meaningful in and of themselves; if so, then concerns about the [consequences of] erosion of U.S. strategic superiority may be unwarranted (Coffey, 1971:37).

> . . . the overall nature of the objective, rather than strategic "superiority," ultimately determines which protagonist will prevail in a crisis (Lambeth, 1972:233).

> . . . regardless of whether you have a nuclear superiority or not, as long as you have the capability to destroy one another, then I don't see why we [Americans] should be less concerned than they are [about nuclear war] . . . (McConnell, Senate Armed Services Committee, 1968:Y4.Ar5/3:P91/27, Pt 2:218).

> Although Soviet superiority in certain static and dynamic measures of nuclear power will eventually ensue . . . "superiority" or asymmetries in the nuclear balance are neither destabilizing nor politically detrimental (Baylis and Segal, 1981:148).

Although the foregoing quotes have been wrenched from contexts rich in details, qualifications, and caveats necessarily omitted here, it can still be seen that the resulting general hypotheses on the relation between force ratios and war cannot coexist.[1] Since Jervis (1976:84-113) is surely correct in arguing that history reveals an embarrassment of confirming and disconfirming instances for deterrence propositions, it is essential to test these propositions to begin to determine if and under what circumstances each holds.

DETERRENCE HYPOTHESES

1) Deterrence works while the status quo power enjoys a lead, while a lead for the revisionist risks war (e.g., Kahn, Kintner, Snyder). This might be expressed (where **D** stands for successful deterrence, **W** for war, **S** for the forces of the status quo power and **R** for those of the revisionist) as the pair of conditionals:

If S > R, then D.
If R > S, then W.

2) Equality between the rival powers promotes peace (e.g., Coffey, Kahn, arms control literature).

If S ≅ R, then D.

3) Equality between the rival powers promotes war (e.g., Kaysen, Pfister).

If S ≅ R, then W.

4) Deterrence works while the revisionist power enjoys a lead, while a lead for the status quo power risks war (Berezhkov, Sokolovsky).

If R > S, then D.
If S > R, then W.

If we assume that there are only three relevant force comparison states, the arguments can be mapped as follows:

TABLE 1
FORCE COMPARISON PREDICTIONS

Force comparison →	S > R implies		S = R implies		S < R implies	
Outcomes	Peace	War	Peace	War	Peace	War
Hypothesis	1	4	2	3	4	1

While each of these hypotheses, with the aid of the appropriate initial conditions and qualifications, may help explain the outcome of particular cases of military rivalry, there exist clear contradictions in the arguments. Hence, it remains to be seen whether any of the hypotheses can be generally confirmed. If they cannot, a large effort to delineate initial conditions under which each hypothesis may hold would be required in subsequent empirical research and theoretical development.

This would not be a meaningless exercise. Divergent views on deterrence have been produced by reasoning from specific historical examples such as Munich and Yalta, searching for modern analogs; by attempting to encompass all logical possibilities via deductive methods of various kinds, with no necessary historical precedents; and by venturing to explain contemporary rapidly changing events on an ad hoc basis. In these efforts a strong influence has been exerted by preconceptions about psychology, history and ideology, and not least by a pervasive ethnocentrism (Booth, 1979). The differences among the variously generated basic deterrence propositions are not accidental or trivial, but represent contemporary and largely competing views. Attempts to confirm or disconfirm these propositions are then meaningful for what they can imply about regularities in bargaining and conflict behavior.

These disparate hypotheses do not necessarily represent any chronological evolution of deterrence thinking or the results of cumulating arguments in the field as a whole, although some authors' work does seem to have developed in this incremental way (Brodie, 1973). Advocates for each para bellum and other view can be found in each of the postwar decades and before, though the vocabulary is altered somewhat in earlier writing. Thus unanimity does not exist on the question of which deterrence hypothesis best describes any given period of world affairs, though there is some tendency for the propositions to reflect the international system characteristics thought to be prevalent at the time of writing. Hence there may be an implicit or explicit assumption that status quo superiority (in the superpower case) corresponded with no superpower war in the 1950s because status quo superiority maintains peace during intervals of significant bipolarity, or during the postwar reconstruction of the revisionist rival, or for other reasons having to do with unspecified or idiosyncratic initial conditions or intervening variables. (See George and Smoke for a discussion of the need to propose bounded rather than unconditional generalizations.) Much deterrence work has this inductive character. It represents to some extent an effort to adapt theory and strategy to the deployment of new weapons, to the increasing political power of military interest groups in many countries, to the emergence of the USSR (and later, the People's

Republic of China) as a major power, and to the proliferation of nuclear weapons, rather than necessarily representing coherent ordered growth.

Another significant portion of deterrence writing has a speculative deductive character, reflecting the deliberations of some authors (Kahn, 1960; Rapoport, 1960; Schelling, 1960) who examine seriatim force ratio-peace relationships without any necessary restrictions to present or probable future scenarios.

DETERRENCE LITERATURE

Some prominent deterrence literature might usefully be ordered in "first, second and third wave" terms (Jervis, 1979), if we understand this classification scheme restrictively to refer to a continuum of increasingly structured arguments rather than to any necessarily chronological order of appearance of the studies, since representative examples from each wave may be found in every period of deterrence writing.

Jervis suggests that first wave deterrence writing was characterized by the formulation of key concepts and by the choice of crucial variables. This also appears to be the period in which powerful assumptions about geopolitical influences and other "world view" questions are made, though they may remain implicit. (Note that there is an important national divergence in the studies at this point, since the Western "Heartland" view holds that the Soviets have a uniquely favored geopolitical position for expansion, while the Soviets hold that the U.S. is in a uniquely favored geopolitical position, both for security and for territorial acquisition.) (Walters, 1974.)

Second wave studies advanced some generalizations and historical applications, again usually highly colored by the nationality of the analysts. Third wave inquiries confronted generalizations with harder evidence. Jervis notes that there is a certain permeability in the classification, since the categories are not mutually exclusive, but build on one another to some extent, with second wave studies depending on the parameters set in the first, and third wave research of necessity deriving from second wave generalizing. If deterrence studies are classified by the highest level of argument evidenced, then a workable classification scheme emerges.

Prominent examples from the deterrence literature then can be arrayed along Jervis' continuum, and presumably across other dimensions reflecting, for example, the prevalent international economic and political system structure, historical and technical factors such as dominant weapons technology and the studied country's position in the projectile cycle.

Here the second dimension used for classification is the number of countries examined in each study. This produces, in principle, a continuum which ranges from zero for studies which are completely abstract to an arbitrarily large number representing the maximum number of nations present or imagined in the system at any point. In practice, deterrence work seems to have ranged from studies which are entirely or essentially abstract, through unitary, dyadic, and multiparty case studies rarely exceeding five or six, to studies which are not case-specific but are drawn from many regions, representing the experiences of a relatively large number of countries.

To the two dimensions produced by the degree of structure in the argument and the sample size, might be added a third dimension (producing a Rubric's Cube), that of time. Some deterrence studies are, in the argument or in the testing, essentially cross-sectional. Others produce hypotheses which are either applicable to a fairly short period, or typical of a brief but arguably cyclical configuration of international system characteristics such as tight bipolarity. A third group sets out generalizations which purport not to be timebound (though the context of testing must be), or to apply at the least in the very long term or to slow-changing international system configurations.

Deterrence thinking is an unevenly developed field, so that there may be some empty cells in the schema showing argument structure, temporal and sample size considerations. The *Trojan Peace* study would be located in the lower right cell (See Table 2). Because the choice of appropriate time span is not always clearly indicated in a particular study, and nation-state referents may be more or less central to the study, there may be some debate about the placement of other work within this rubric. Nevertheless this classification schema can serve to set *Trojan Peace* in context within the deterrence literature, using some representative works such as a third wave, multinational, long-term study.

Some third wave multinational research is summarized here so that apparent consistencies in the empirical findings may be highlighted. Naroll (1969) argues in a comparative case study of major states ("conspicuous states" and "conspicuous rivals") that preparing for war has not appeared historically to make peace more likely. In particular, he shows that in a sample of dominant civilizations, four types of military advantage in the status quo power failed to be correlated (linearly) with nation-months of war in the period of status quo nation superiority. If the para bellum view had been upheld, a strong negative relation would have been expected. The types of status quo advantage which did *not* appear to promote peace were larger armed forces, more mobile armed forces, better quality armed forces and more extensive fortifications.

TABLE 2

A CLASSIFICATION OF DETERRENCE LITERATURE USING SOME REPRESENTATIVE EXAMPLES

	Abstract, no country referent necessary	Specific to one country	Specific to a dyad	Multinational sample of cases	
First Wave	Wolfers (1962)				cross-sectional
		Garthoff (1962) Mirchandani (1968) Morley (1976)	Kahn (1960)	Huntington (1958)	short-term
			Lambeth (1972) Walters (1974)	Brodie (1973)	long-term
Second Wave	Schelling (1960, 66) Ellsberg (1961) Rapoport (1960, 64)				cross-sectional
	" Legault and Lindsey (1974)	Jabber (1971) Subrahmanyam (1974) Whiting (1975)	Douglass and Hoeber (1976) Coffey (1971) Wohlstetter (1959)	Jervis (1976) Quester (1977)	short-term
	Booth (1979) Deutsch (1968)	Goldhamer (1971)	George and Smoke (1974) Snyder (1961) Sokolovsky (1975)	Smoke (1978)	long-term
Third Wave			Doran (1973)	Naroll (1969)	cross-sectional
		Jones (1974b) Russett (1967) Voevodsky (1972)	Saris and Middendorp (1980)	Fink (1965) Russett (1963) Wright (1965)	short-term
				Naroll (1974) Smith (1982) Wallace (1980, 1981)	long-term

25

In a more comprehensive study (Naroll, Bullough and Naroll, 1974) twenty conspicuous states, analogous to major powers, well distributed through the preindustrial era and across the planet were examined. To test a basic para bellum hypothesis, the authors examined whether war was less frequent when status quo powers (their "states in a defensive stance") possessed military advantages vis-a-vis their rival states. Measures of military superiority again included larger armed forces, more mobile armed forces, better quality forces and extensive fortifications. The 1974 results show little support for the deterrent value of superior military establishments. Status quo powers obtaining larger armies than their rivals conferred no particular advantage on themselves; war was then about as likely as when status quo powers' armies were smaller than their rivals'. Status quo powers with more mobile forces than their rivals' were actually *more* likely to go to war than if they had less mobility. However, this relationship is not especially powerful. The point biserial correlation is .26 and the one-tailed t test of significance yields .14 (Naroll, et al., 1974:329). Better quality forces among status quo powers is also positively associated with war frequency, though this result is not particularly significant statistically. The only support for para bellum deterrence propositions here lies in the observation that fortifications appear negatively, albeit weakly, linked to war frequency. This would argue for the deterrent function of essentially defensive ventures, except that the significance level here (.25) is not altogether persuasive (Naroll, et al., 1974:329).

In sum, in the 1974 study there is again no support for the deterrent value of some major types of military advantage to the status quo power, and the only relatively significant relationship showed that having easy-to-deploy mobile forces is correlated with an *increase* in war frequency. (Advocates of Rapid Deployment Forces take heed.) Similar results obtained in related but somewhat less relevant studies of war preparation in developing societies (Naroll, 1964; Naroll, et al., 1971). Low but *positive* correlations are shown between war frequency and military readiness. Thus in the Naroll investigations there is no real support for any of the hypothesized deterrence relations which imply that status quo superiority yields peace. However, the authors do show that quality (that is, amount of training, not size or mobility) of armed forces serves a *defense* advantage function, though not a deterrence function. Armed forces quality has been moderately well-related, not to war prevention, but to territorial gain once war begins (point biserial correlation = .37, significant at .06, in Naroll, 1974:337).

In international relations there has been relatively little quantitative work directly bearing on contemporary deterrence questions. Two examples from early empirical work on deterrence show equivocal results, but tend to point toward a disconfirmation of the hypothesis that status quo superiority (local or at higher levels) is associated with peace. In investigating when a threat by a defender nation against an aggressor prevents attack on a "pawn" country, Fink (1965) shows no characteristics common to all cases of unsuccessfully deterred attack, but finds, for all the *no attack* (deterrence success) cases (n = 6, 1945-1961), where the defender was either the nuclear armed U.S. or the nuclear armed USSR, the defender did *not* possess local military superiority over the potential attacker. At the strategic level, Russett (1963) shows, depending on the count, that either five or seven of eleven attack (deterrence failure) cases in his study are cases in which the defender had strategic superiority over the attacker. While Russett may have established a (weak) tendency for status quo strategic superiority to be associated with deterrence failure ($7/11 \cong .63$), results in this range are about what would be expected in a large number of cases over time if in fact there were no simple relation between the defender's superiority and deterrence failure.

The rough parity hypotheses have also been examined in some quantitative international relations research on war origins. Singer, Bremer and Stuckey (1972) show that rough parity in capabilities, and change toward rough parity, are associated with less war in the nineteenth century, while this relation appeared to vanish in the twentieth century with the advent of new technology and arguably different decision-making methods.

Parity is presumed to be peace related because, depending on weapons and on defense systems, it may provide minimum available incentives for preempting, short of disarmament. On the other hand, clear superiority for one rival as evinced by large numerical differences or other advantages between force levels might be expected to be war related because in some circumstances each side has an incentive to preempt: the superior side because it may be confident of victory; and the inferior side because, by preempting, it gains its only advantage—surprise. The Correlates of War project finds that 34 of 50 inter-state wars studied were won by initiators, documenting a widespread belief in the military advantage of preempting, at least in nonnuclear conflicts (Singer and Small, 1972).

In more recent and more technically sophisticated analyses of the para bellum question, Wallace has shown a set of consistent findings using Correlates of War data. Wallace's findings converged on the discovery that arms racing indices continue to be better predictors of the onset of war than are the usual deterrence-specified force ratios. In Wallace (1972), rapid arms growth in a five year period was associated not with a damping of hostilities but with an increase in the magnitude of war in the subsequent period. Later (1979) Wallace computes an arms race index based on smoothed growth rates in armaments over a decade, and demonstrates that disputes erupting between rivals with high scores on the arms race index are more likely to end in war than are disputes between adversaries with lower racing scores. (See also Wallace, 1980.) In 1980 and 1981 Wallace brings out the deterrence relevance of his work even more explicitly by comparing, via joint logit estimation analysis, the predictive power of three indices of military superiority and differential growth in arming (some interpretations of "para bellum") versus the predictive power of an arms racing index. Superiority is examined here in two senses, both as simple ratios of military outlays and as ratios of growth rates. Thus, for one application, Wallace reasons:

> If the para bellum hypothesis is in fact the correct explanation, then the onset of lethal conflict should be proceeded [sic] by a relatively rapid rate of arms growth on the part of the challenging or "revisionist" power, and a relatively slower rate of growth on the part of the "status quo" power. Thus, the ratio of [the] two ratios of growth ought to be a better predictor of war outcome . . . (Wallace, 1981:92).

But in these data none of the para bellum indices is as useful a predictor as is the arms racing indicator; the others are not significant. Wallace concludes:

> . . . whatever other problems it may have caused, war has not been rendered more probable solely by virtue of a revisionist state possessing or threatening to possess military superiority; conversely, merely by maintaining and guarding its superiority, a status quo power does nothing to reduce the risk of war (Wallace, 1981:94).

In a nonquantitative assessment of deterrence in the MIRV era, Lambeth echoes Wallace's findings:

> . . . the actual behavior of the U.S. during the [Cuban Missile] crisis suggested anything but confidence that our superiority would bring us through unscathed . . . In none of the three cases . . . did the strategic nuclear balance play any significant role . . . (Lambeth, 1972:232-33).

Wallace's analyses and those presented below, based on a distinct data set and different indicators, show that the force relations conventionally called upon to preserve the peace have not had a major role historically in serving this function.

CONTEXT OF TESTING: ARMS RACING

Here it has been assumed that not all war years and not all peace years bring useful information to bear on the general question of military postures as deterrents, but only those years of war and peace which are part of a period of hostile or competitive foreign policy and appear to show interactive arming patterns. In such periods some conflict of objectives exists between rivals, hence some dissuasion—i.e., deterrence—of intended but high risk acts may be presumed. It is, of course, possible that deterrence calculations only affect policymaking sporadically, or discontinuously, i.e., when major production decisions must be made (Saris and Middendorp, 1980); but if deterrence functions consistently, it should be highly visible during arms racing intervals. Although there is inevitably some mix of defense and deterrent strategies behind these competitions, except in clear cases of predator-prey rivalries in which one side is at a profound disadvantage, the deterrent aspect of arming would be heightened over the defense function during racing. And even in the predatory war cases, the initiator may use deterrence to time the onset of war propitiously. Preemption is an added advantage to a superior adversary in some circumstances, while it may be an inferior adversary's only edge. Thus greatly disadvantaged nations cannot be counted on not to preempt even though their defeat seems assured, as per Japan in 1941. From this stems a potential need to deter in arms racing. This apparent although not necessarily successful *deterrent* character of arms racing may be especially evident in nuclear arms races, since the feasibility of a real nuclear defense is doubtful, and there is no such defense now. Thus the present context of testing is an appropriate one and perhaps one in which deterrence should be maximally conspicuous.

If deterrence propositions are most applicable to periods of declared animosity in foreign policy or competition for the same objectives, and to periods of military rivalry, implying the existence of both *potentially deterrable hostile acts* and of the *means, continually elaborated, to carry out these acts and/or retribution for them* on both sides, then hypotheses on the working of deterrence would be well tested in a sample of arms race data. For this context of testing to be useful, arms racing must be well defined, to capture both the military competition and some indication of its political objectives, considering arms racing as internationally targeted behavior rather than as an entirely domestically driven process. (For arguments on the domestic pressure factor, see Tufte, 1973; Wohlstetter, 1974; Gray, 1976; Saris and Middendorp, 1980. For a sketch of a counterargument, see Appendix II.)

Here an arms race is defined as apparently competitive or interactive increases in quantity or quality of war material, or of persons under arms. In this analysis races are all treated as dyadic, usually pairing nation-states with other nation-states, but occasionally, where this seems justified by the foreign policy statements of the racers, coupling a nation-state against an alliance or some set of adversary states. For some purposes it may be reasonable to alter the composition of racing groups in mid-race when major adversary or decision calculi changes are made (Moll, 1974). Here, for the sake of simplicity, this possibility is ignored.

For the purposes of these analyses, then, the unit of analysis is national participation in arms racing over the years designated as arms race intervals for a given country. This national participation is operationalized as national military expenditures (in various forms), over the years in which these expenditures are generally rising, and hostility against some specifically identified rival has been declared. National participation in arms racing then consists of a period of increasing military expenditures, at the beginning of which statements of intent of government officials indicate (if taken at face value) that the military expansion envisioned is funded in response to or in anticipation of antagonistic behavior on the part of a perceived or potential adversary. Although arms racing appears to be atypical behavior for states, historically, arms racing has apparently enjoyed some popularity in the racing countries. Since few penalties have attached to announcements of evidently competitive military programs, such statements have been fairly straightforward: "Peru pursued no other objective than . . . to erase Chile from the waters of the Pacific" (Diplomatic notes cited in Barros, 1970:278-79). Chile then ordered some new ironclad ships "para equilibrar nuestro Poderío naval" (Barros, 1970:245), i.e., to "balance" our naval power, according to the Chilean Council of Ministers.

Determining duration of arms races entails considerable difficulty. First, the question of arms racing continuing through wars arises (Steiner, 1973). There are examples of arms races—such as the British one from 1894-1907 (Moll, 1974) and the ongoing Soviet-American one—which are punctuated by wars (the Boer War, Vietnam), yet which clearly continue against the major rival without major perturbation. Therefore it seems misleading to consider going to war with *any* nation as indicating the end of all races in which any of the belligerents may have been previously involved. If the first two conditions set forth below for ending a race are also met, here wars of self-declared adversaries mark the end of any arms race involving only the warring parties. (Races may and do end in other ways.) This designation of the end of a race seems reasonable because, as Voevodsky (1969) and others have noted, once war begins, combat attrition and logistical considerations begin to obscure the initial rivalry of weapons accumulation, and to transform the underlying decision calculi into competition to minimize the ratio of one's own to enemy casualties, or some other indicator of altered and more immediately pressing goals.

Beginning of Arms Racing. Two conditions for the beginning of arms racing are specified: (1) Some statement that the country in question is adapting its arming behavior to conform to or to anticipate actions of an adversary or potential rival is required. This condition, positing a budgetary response to a perceived threat, could be met by either or both of two government statements. A statement of intent to change current levels of military power relative to a rival (regardless of how power is measured in the statement) must be made publicly in year t_0, the arms race starting year, and must be represented as official foreign or defense policy by a military or government representative; or a response by a country or countries acknowledging such a challenge, expressing intent to "meet or surpass" it, or to "maintain superiority" (Reagan's "margin of safety") in the face of a threat (real or imagined) must be recorded. (2) A definite increase in current price local currency military spending must be noted. (It is assumed that political leaders perceive their military expenditures primarily in their own currencies and base arming decisions on these perceptions. However, the statistical analyses are conducted using U.S. dollar figures, reflecting an implicit price deflator for government purchases.[2] Inspection showed that had the arms race intervals been identified using deflated dollars, most of the same arms racing years would have been identified.)

Generally, the requirement of an increase in spending to identify the beginning of an arms race in year t_0 was expressed as either (a) a positive change in the slope of the spending curve in year t_0 or t_1 must be observed, where in years t_{-2} and t_{-1} the slope is zero or positive but less than that obtained in year t_0 or t_1; or (b) the slope of military spending must become positive in year t_0 or t_1, having been negative in years t_{-2} and t_{-1}.

End of Arms Racing. An arms race is over when both (or all) participants stop racing. As mentioned earlier, a war between racers marks the end of their arms race. Otherwise, two sufficient conditions for the end of participation in arms racing are: (1) a notable decrease in expenditure must occur, or (2) there must be no reasonable grounds for finding a qualitative arms race (in which major innovations might be introduced without necessarily being reflected in the budget), extraordinary sources of funding for the military, and/or evidence that official expenditure figures are fraudulent, or accurate but incomplete. More specifically, a "notable" decrease is evidenced when the slope of a participant's military expenditure curve becomes negative in year t_x from positive values or zero in year t_{x-1}, unless available information indicates that spending is being erroneously reported. Falling expenditures must persist for at least two periods if they alone—rather than war or a less exciting denouement in foreign policy—mark the end of the race.

Regardless of spending patterns, an arms race is also ended by definition when: (1) war breaks out between the racing rivals, (2) genuine ententes or alliances are signed between competitors, (3) rapprochement occurs, and is evidenced in either no more hostile government statements, or a predominance of friendly statements, or no necessary proclamation of altered policy, but observed and reported changes in provocations abroad (e.g., determined effort to avoid border incidents, cessation of military raids sent into rival countries, as per Indonesia and Malaysia).

If any of these events occurs, the last year of the race is determined according to the month in which the event took place. If such an event took place in the first six months of a year, that year is considered outside the arms race, and the prior year is counted as the last year of the ongoing military rivalry. If war began in the last six months of a given year, the entire year is considered the last year of that particular arms race.

Given these criteria for beginning and ending of arms races, the competitions were identified through this procedure:

1) To produce longitudinal records of military outlays, information from several sources was pooled. For the period since World War II the Stockholm International Peace Research Institute (SIPRI) World Armaments and Disarmament *Yearbooks* and the U.S. Arms Control and Disarmament Agency (ACDA) publications on global military expenditures were consulted. From 1860 forward, Banks' *Cross Polity Time Series Data* military spending figures are incorporated with those from the *Statesman's Yearbook* and the *Almanach de Gotha*, where Banks shows missing or apparently incompletely reported spending data. For 1850 to 1859, the *Statesman's Yearbook* and the *Almanach*, which take their expenditure figures from published national budgets and show some actual expenditure records, are used alone.

Since Banks relies on the *Statesman's Yearbook* as the principle source of government expenditures for 1860-1939 (Banks, 1971:19), the *Cross-Polity* source is used simply for the convenience of having the *Statesman's Yearbook* figures already compiled. A separate search of the original figures in the *Statesman's Yearbook* suggests that the errors in Banks' military data in this period may be mainly those of omission. These errors have been remedied by recourse to the sources cited in the preceding paragraph.

This search produced a continuous compilation of military outlays for 1850-1977, beginning roughly when reliable budgetary data first became available world wide.

2) A list of all increasing sequences of at least four years appearing in the spending data from about 1850 to 1977 was compiled. This yielded 200 candidate arms races for various nations, using no maximum length, and a lower cutoff point of four years' minimum duration for a candidate arms race.

3) The diplomatic histories of countries showing such candidate races were examined in multiple sources for evidence of hostile or competitive foreign policies. When these policies could be identified, when a target was named and when the military spending pattern of the target nation met the arms race criteria, an arms race was demarcated.

Using the procedure outlined, working first from the spending data and then searching the historical record, the author obtained a list of thirty-two arms races (see Table 3) with racers' foreign policy (revisionist or status quo) indicated.

TABLE 3
ARMS RACES 1860-1977

Racers*	Years	Outcome	Comments
1. China (SQ) vs England and France (RV)	1860-1874	War	(Omitted from analyses because of inadequate data)
2. Chile (RV) vs Peru (SQ)	1868-1879	War	
3. Guatemala (RV) vs El Salvador (SQ)	1877-1885	War	(Guatemala racing either alone or after El Salvador stopped)
4. Greece (RV) vs Turkey (SQ)	1880-1896	War	

Racers	Years	Outcome	Comments
5. China (SQ) vs Japan (RV)	1885–1894	War	(Omitted from statistical analyses because data inadequate)
6. Norway (RV) vs Sweden (SQ)	1895–1905	Peace	
7. Russia vs Japan	1896–1903	War	(Omitted because of complex foreign policies)
8. England (SQ) vs Germany (RV)	1898–1914	War	
9. Turkey (SQ) vs Serbia (RV) and Bulgaria (RV)	1899–1912	War	
10. France (RV) vs Germany (SQ)	1904–1914	War	
11. Russia (SQ) vs Japan (RV)	1907–1914	Race Re-entered	
12. Russia (SQ) vs Japan (RV)	1921–1938	War	
13. England and the US (SQ) vs Japan (RV)	1921–1940	War	
14. Bolivia vs Paraguay	1924–1932	War	(Omitted: both revisionists? Data inadequate)
15. Finland (RV) vs USSR (SQ)	1930–1938	War	
16. Britain (SQ) vs Germany (RV)	1934–1939	War	
17. USSR (SQ) vs Germany (RV)	1934–1940	War	
18. France (SQ) vs Germany (RV)	1936–1939	War	
19. U.S. (SQ) vs USSR (RV)	1949–1977	Continuing	
20. Israel (SQ) vs Arabs (RV)	1949–1955	War	
21. Israel (SQ) vs Arabs (RV)	1957–1966	War	

Racers	Years	Outcome	Comments
22. Israel (SQ) vs Arabs (RV)	1968–1973	War	
23. India (SQ) vs Pakistan (RV)	1957–1964	War	
24. India (SQ) vs Pakistan (RV)	1966–1971	War	
25. Iran (SQ) vs Iraq (RV)	1958–1973	Peace	(Temporarily; subsequent war apparently more closely tied to unresolved territorial and other issues than to prior arming)
26. USSR (SQ) vs PRC (RV)	1959–1977	Continuing	
27. Indonesia (SQ) vs Malaysia (RV)	1961–1966	Rapprochement	
28. South Africa (SQ) vs OAU (RV)	1961–1977	Continuing	
29. North (RV) vs South Korea (RV)	1962–1977	Continuing	
30. France (RV) vs Germany (SQ)	1964–1977	Continuing	
31. India (SQ) vs PRC (RV)	1964–1977	Continuing	
32. Albania (RV) vs USSR (SQ)	1968–1977	Continuing	

*Foreign policy designations: SQ – status quo
RV – revisionist, challenger

Gray (1971, 1976), Huntington (1958), Moll (1974) and others have tentatively identified selections of arms races in prior studies. The definition of racing used here resulted in the inclusion of different years and in some cases of different racers than in those cases identified previously, and also greatly expanded the sample.

Deterrence Success. For the purposes of this investigation, successful deterrence in a given year of arms racing will mean that war did not break out in that year between the competitors themselves. Wars with or through other parties ("proxy wars") are ignored, as are all other foreign political moves short of war, including the superpowers' quasi-clandestine intelligence "wars" (Cox, 1976). Presumably the complexities of actual military planning are designed for defense as well as for deterrence, and in part to deter a broader range of events perceived as aggressive, but here the focus is on the hypothesized direct deterrence of war between military rivals. This definitional limitation to rival/rival wars makes sense especially in view of recent arguments to the effect that modern strategic weaponry has little defense value and cannot be expected to deter "brushfire" or system-peripheral wars, insurrections, revolutions or invasions (with the arguable exception of those in Central Europe), or indeed to deter successfully any general class of events except major power war. (See, for instance, Halperin, 1963.) The possibilities that arms racing serves some other deterrence functions at a lower level, or that it plays crucial domestic roles, are not examined here. (See Appendix II.)

Force Comparisons: Parity. There has been some tendency in the West to define parity as a state in which rivals possess roughly equal offensive forces, or highly similar strategic forces. This usage is also adopted in the SALT treaty and drafts, with some attempt to show equality in numbers of some delivery vehicles. However, parity in this sense is a difficult term to apply since obtaining intersubjective agreement as to when parity exists in any given rivalry presents great difficulty. These difficulties may be maximized in the U.S.-USSR case. Not only is there no objective way to label most hardware "offensive" or "defensive," because these terms apply fundamentally not to the objects themselves but to the circumstances of their use, there also exists a long-standing difference between Western and Eastern usage of the terms "strategic" and "tactical." Thus the types of force to be included in the count cannot be objectively determined since, for illustration, small nuclear weapons in Europe which the U.S. regards as tactical can present a threat to the European USSR "homeland" (and to virtually all of the USSR when long-range cruise missiles are deployed), making American "tactical" nuclear weapons in Europe "strategic" to the Soviets. (See the SALT definitions accompanying the draft treaty.)

A second use of the term "parity" has it that parity exists when rivals possess unequal but still significant, mutually "unacceptably damaging" strike-back abilities. ("Strike-back" is Snyder's [1961] vivid synonym for "second strike.") This definition relies on each rival's highly subjective estimate of his adversary's threshold of "unacceptable damage" in any particular case, for any particular objective; it also relies crucially on the odds of achieving this unacceptable damage at any instant. Additionally, such a definition of parity relies directly on experimental evidence for weapons performance which may be strictly classified and may not be widely available outside major and regional powers. In the nuclear case, weapons performance estimates may be less than enlightening, since a serious isomorphism problem is presented by extending performance estimates from peacetime to wartime conditions, in view of electromagnetic disturbances in the atmosphere in the vicinity of a detonation, etc. So this use of "parity" can only be applied to a restricted group of contenders, and is not a generally applicable one. There are major uncertainties at several levels in the actual application of the term, even in the appropriate and well-documented cases. This uncertainty is increased if we assume that compensation occurs across weapons systems or even across the nuclear/conventional line, so that vulnerabilities in one area may be made up in some other(s).

Still another use of "parity" has to do with the complex interaction of defensive and offensive forces and command and control systems. For this purpose, parity exists if the confrontation of A's offensive forces with B's defenses would probably yield surviving forces (or cities) which are roughly comparable to B's forces (or cities) surviving an offensive against A's defenses.

Variants on these three central definitions of parity also exist, and answer various theoretical purposes. They all have the virtue of relying at least at the outset on empirical facts about hardware in the national arsenal.

In the present set of analyses, parity is understood as rough equality in military budgets, since budget data are argued to provide a good surrogate measure for hardware (Abolfathi, 1975). Since the difficulties in compiling information for the application of psychologically determined or geographically relative definitions of parity to a wide range of international rivalries appear intractable at present, and definitions based on counterfactual assumptions are even more troublesome (even though at some point a hardware-based study is essential), the budget data may now provide the best generally available measure of force standing. It is true that this budget measure relies on some economic assumptions concerning comparative value of labor, etc., but these contentions are more clearly understood than are their psychological counterparts and appear to be falsifiable; thus, they are preferable.[3] This rough budget equality measure may also be appropriate because it allows compensation across categories of weaponry and personnel, as is generally agreed to take place in military policy planning, so that an advantage in number of ICBMs might be compensated for by an advantage in quality of submarines and accuracy of submarine-launched missiles.

Force Comparisons: Superiority. "Superiority" is used in the literature in several senses. It may refer to qualitative differences such as the apparent U.S. lead in electronics vis-a-vis the Soviets, or may refer to quantitative differences between rivals' forces. Where quantitative differences are referred to, there appear to be no real parameters distinguishing significant from insignificant differences, other than case-specific ones, except in the event that one rival possesses the ability to strike a disarming blow. Since the literature appears not to prescribe the margins of superiority which may be generally meaningful for deterrence except in the first strike case (itself ambiguous), no particular requirement is imposed in this study. Instead, any positive differences between rivals which appear to be statistically notable are reported in the results.

Since force levels are measured here in budgetary (deflated dollar) terms, superiority for one adversary in a given year is a military budget which exceeds that of the opponent. Superior rates of change are also discussed, as are superior ratio measures. Inferiority is shown in a particular year by a smaller military budget, or smaller ratios or rates of change. (In this context see the controversy surrounding U.S. CIA Team A vs. Team B's assessment of the appropriate comparison to be made between American and Soviet defense outlays.) Note that this is a summary measure of force standing and does not take into account qualitative differences or the separate comparisons of performance for different branches of the armed forces or of particular weapons or defense and communications systems. Case studies make a valuable contribution at this level.

This military budget measure of superiority, like those used by Wallace (1981) and Russett (1964), is an indicator of general preponderance across categories of weapons and types of armed forces. It does not necessarily capture the above-mentioned aspect of definitions of superiority occasionally used in the deterrence literature—the ability to strike a "disarming" blow—although there may be some tendency historically for powers which are superior in one sense to be superior in the other as well.

Since it is possible to imagine circumstances in which, with forces which were palpably inferior in number, size or sophistication, a subordinate state could strike a disarming blow against a vastly superior adversary who had, for example, inadvisedly left his forces concentrated, the disarming blow criterion yields classifications in which a state could be both superior and inferior at the same time. Thus the disarming blow idea seems definitionally inadequate. It appears to refer not to the relative force balance directly, but to risk factors which modify the force balance (via estimates of probable surviving forces), which are time-constrained, and which are entailed by certain attack or deployment modes and technological advancements coupled with limitations on effective defense, i.e., some of the calculations behind a first strike.

The need for a definitional distinction between force ratios per se and willingness/ability to try for a decisive first strike is illustrated by the case of Japan in the 1940s. A manifestly inferior Japan went to war in 1941, banking on dealing a devastating early blow and hoping for a consequently early settlement. Clearly, an inferior adversary hoping to roll high and therefore willing to accept large risks—even those of preemption—is not converted into a superior adversary by virtue of a risk-accepting strategy. This confusion arises because of the historical partial coincidence between preemption and achieving prewar goals, as well as because of the association in some deterrence thinking between superiority and preemption. However, it is not necessarily a superior power which preempts, as Jervis notes, as long as cost tolerance is high:

> It does not take a superior or even an equal military force to show by limited use that one is willing to take extreme measures rather than suffer defeat . . . a reminder that superior military capability does not guarantee deterrence is provided by the Japanese decision to go to war in 1941 . . . they knew perfectly well that they could not win an all-out [protracted] war. [But they were not expecting to have to fight such a war. . .] (Jervis, 1980:632-33).

This is another way to say that an inferior state may attempt a disarming strike or short, intense war with low probability of success, without confidence that it will avoid unacceptable damage, if the alternative appears grim enough. Thus the appearance of the ability to attempt a disarming strike is not necessarily an indicator of superiority, if only because an entirely successful disarming strike probably exists only in theory, so this criterion is not adopted in the definition of superiority applied here.

A cross-national study which analyzed deterrence propositions via estimates of probable surviving forces instead of general comparisons between aggregate force levels would make an important contribution to empirical assessments of deterrence thinking. But such a study would require case-specific historical estimates based on a variety of battle scenarios for each arms racer, and deriving from a congeries of assumptions about performance which are more complex and more subjective than those employed here. (See Rapoport's [1960] critique of the deterrence use of "probability" to mean "degree of subjective belief.") For these reasons, the measures of general preponderance are adopted here as the best overall indicators of superiority for international comparisons over time.

"Status Quo" and "Revisionist" Powers. In practice there may be great difficulty in determining which state should be designated the status quo power, as much "revisionism" and much defense of the "status quo" lies in the eyes of the beholder. However, because many major deterrence hypotheses are couched in these terms, some designations must be made to test the hypotheses. The assumption in the literature frequently is that deterrence propositions only apply to circumstances in which there is a clear challenger and an unambiguous status quo power, or a would-be "attacker" and a "defender," intersubjectively identified.

For the purposes of these analyses the arms racers in the sample for whom adequate budgetary data exist are labelled revisionists (challengers) or status quo powers in the way generally indicated by Wallace (1980), according to the author's judgment of their foreign policies toward one another, based on several diplomatic histories. These designations have been incorporated into the list of arms races in Table 3.

To determine whether one country was essentially revisionist or essentially status quo in its foreign policies toward a rival state, two aspects of their relations are examined: public opinion (subjective); and existing foreign policy interests at issue (objective). That a country was a revisionist power vis-a-vis another at a particular time could be evidenced by showing that the attentive public, or the political decision makers, or both, preferred or advocated a major change in relations with a foreign country, and that political decision makers were actively planning or carrying out measures to bring about the desired alterations over specific issues of contention. An example may clarify the procedure and the nature of the evidence sought to make the case.

Japan is shown to be the revisionist party in the Far Eastern race with Britain and the U.S. (number 13) by virtue of reports of Japanese public opinion during and just prior to the arms race, by the apparent preferences and policies of Japanese and Western decision makers and by an examination of the foreign interests which were at stake. Taking this last question first, Taylor (1961:215) unambiguously labels the Japanese the "aggressor" power in this particular contention, for reasons which are fairly crude and longstanding:

1) The United Kingdom and the U.S. had established naval supremacy in the area, to guarantee territorial and commercial claims;

2) Japan was building up her navy with the explicitly stated plan of altering the established Western naval preponderance (Crowley, 1966:26). See also the annual National Defense Policy statements for Japan;

3) The United Kingdom held (besides Singapore) Shanghai and Hong Kong;

4) Beginning in 1931 with the occupation of Manchuria, Japan expanded its de facto control of China, threatening established British interests.

By 1938-1939 Japanese forces controlled all of the Chinese coast (Taylor, 1961:125), with consequent challenge to British holdings.

Thus in foreign policy the questions at issue—besides that of territorial change by force—were naval preponderance and control of colonies, as well as resource and financial matters stemming from the colonies. In these matters the Japanese political leaders, apparently supported by domestic public opinion, advocated and to some extent achieved a revision in the international status quo, partly as a result of events in Europe, including the West's neglect of Japan's prior claims:

> As Ōhata (Tokushirō) points out, Ōshima and (German Foreign Minister) Ribbentrop desired a German-Japanese alliance. Such an alliance was also promoted by some elements in the Japanese military and by the so-called Shiratori faction within the Foreign Ministry; and it was supported by a growing body of ultranationalist writers, who helped create a national mood of dissatisfaction with the international status quo. (Taiheiyō sensō e no michi: kaisen gaikō shi, trans. and ed. Morley, 1976:4-5).

Naturally this case can also be argued from a Japanese perspective to reverse the status quo-revisionist labels. Then, of course, the Manchurian occupation and the expansion through China were precipitated by the failure of the international community to protect Japanese commercial interests rather like the European ones in China. If the European holdings in China were illegitimate to begin with, then the British (and American) navies' presence was aggressive, reviving Japan's real concerns of encirclement. Thus there developed a genuinely perceived need for the Japanese forces to respond to the "aggression" of outside powers from another hemisphere, to restore the status quo *ante*. In this case, I have followed Borg, et al: (1973), Morley (1976), Taylor (1961) and others in determining Japan to be the revisionist power. Throughout the case studies, attempts have been made to circumvent some of the arbitrariness in these foreign policy designations by focusing mainly on disputes contemporary with the arms race under study, ignoring prior historical grievances where this seems possible or reasonable, since the choice among historical benchmarks used to mark off periods of status quo or revisionist policies is strongly affected by nationalism.

Where it has not been possible to make an unambiguous case for a unique status quo and revisionist power in each arms race, the race is removed from the analyses. Thus the possibility of examining deterrence of war between two status quo or two revisionist powers is excluded at the outset, as it appears to be in the bulk of deterrence writing.

Perhaps the American-Soviet case deserves special comment, since it can easily be argued, from a Soviet perspective though not exactly in their terms, that the USSR is a "status quo" power content with the general trend of global social change, and with the world "correlation of forces." The U.S., on the other hand, would be a "revisionist" country which not only intervened to try to topple the early Soviet government but has ever since stood in the way of the "normal development of progressive governments" around the world. This apparent contradictory use of the terms is produced partly by the contrast in American vs. Soviet understanding of the term "status quo," since the customary American use is a static one and the Soviets' is dynamic; i.e., the Soviets tend to discuss favorable directions of change. Here, for consistency with the Western literature, the USSR is regarded as a revisionist country.

War. War is defined as per Singer and Small. This definition includes all nonimperial and noncolonial deadly quarrels 1816-1965 which took place between or among sovereign countries whose populations were at least 500,000 and whose battle casualties reached 1,000. (Numbers of civilian casualties and delayed military fatalities are known with too little precision to be used in this definition.) The updated Singer and Small compilation of international wars was used, and their criteria applied to extend the list to conflicts occurring after the Correlates of War (COW) reports were made. According to my information, the additional wars which meet the Singer-Small definitional criteria for 1965-1977 are:

1) Arab-Israeli War (1967);
2) War between Honduras and El Salvador (1969);
3) India-Pakistani Confrontation (1971);
4) Arab-Israeli War (1973).

There are alternate definitions, operationalizations and catalogs of wars (e.g., Richardson, Wright, and Sorokin), but Singer and Small have provided the most extensive one to date.

Initiation of war between arms racers which meets the COW criteria is defined as deterrence failure. Wars accepted for these analyses can then be identified in Singer and Small's *Wages of War: A Statistical Handbook* with the four additions cited above.

SPECIFICATION OF HYPOTHESES

While the deterrence literature points to relative force standing between contending powers as an indication of probable deterrent success, it does not give much theoretical guidance on either the form of the relationship or on the operationalizations of force standing which are to be preferred. Since the mathematical form of the relationship is theoretically unspecified, it seems wise to choose a technique which makes relatively few assumptions about the dependent-independent variable relationship. As is further discussed in the methods section, logit analysis might be the most appropriate choice in this context, but this option is locally unavailable. Discriminant function analysis appears to be the next best method, since the independent variables' relation to the dependent variable need not be strictly linear for the technique to predict well where relationships do exist (Cleary, 1980; Klecka, 1980).

Taking the second question of operationalizations, and assuming that budgetary data provide an accurate measure of forces (Abolfathi, 1975) as well as of commitment to arms racing, the choice of the precise configurations which the spending data should take to reflect deterrence decision-making calculi remains fairly arbitrary. These configurations then may be selected to reflect scholarly use and political application.

There seem to be at least three basic themes in discussions of deterrence and arms racing questions which appear to be operative in decision making and which should be reflected in the measures of force standing. These include:

1) Absolute values of differences in several terms between rivals, which may create pressures to preempt. (There is historical evidence that competitors monitor any apparent force differences closely. See Crowley [1966:26] for Japanese plans to "maintain supremacy" over the U.S. in the Pacific in 1920.)

2) Ratios of forces showing advantage or disadvantage between rivals and approximating "catching-up" distances or margins of superiority.

43

3) Rates of change and relative advantage or differences in rates of change (e.g., differential modernization).

These relative comparisons appear to be used in military policy making. (See, for example, British First Lord of the Admiralty McKenna's accepted and financed proposal in 1909 to outbuild German dreadnoughts by an 8/4 ratio [Albertini, 1982], p. 323). In foreign policy making generally, Carr observes:

> . . . foreign policy never can or never should, be divorced from strategy. The foreign policy of a country is limited not only by its aims, but also by its military strength, or, more accurately, by the ratio of its military strength to that of other countries (Carr, 1946:110).

Force ratios might be expected to be war related since such calculations affect estimated probability of winning an objective via war and to some extent determine the cost of the objective.

Since neither absolute levels of arming nor differences between rivals captures the essentially dynamic aspect of arming for deterrence, rates of change in racing should be tested as well as static indicators. Richardson (1960a, 1960b), Voevodsky (1969, 1970, 1972) and others treat this dynamic process idea theoretically, and Wallace (1980) provides examples of an interesting operationalization in index form. An appeal to the importance for deterrence of rates of change in arming can also be inferred from allegations in the 1979 U.S. congressional hearings on SALT II that even if the U.S. may now exhibit clear superiority over the USSR in some areas, because of differing rates of arming and anticipated changes in these rates, the U.S. will be faced with a projected "window of vulnerability" in ICBMs in the early 1980s, against which the U.S. was urged to prepare in 1979.

Rapid rates of change in arming might be expected to characterize war-prone periods, because rapid accumulation of even familiar weapons and the introduction of new ones produce uncertainties, of which this possibly fictitious "window of vulnerability" could be one. The connection between accelerated arming and deterrence failure would also be expected because of the perceptual problems induced by additional uncertainty (Zinnes, 1968), because of the heightened risk of war by technical accident in accelerating racing, and because of the possibly greater frequency of and less flexible handling of international crises under such circumstances (Herman, 1972; Holsti, 1972).

When rates of change are introduced in various ways, and arming as an economic effort is considered, several comparisons of force standing can be produced to measure different kinds of alleged advantage. These measures to be used to predict deterrence success are described as follows where:

MX   represents military expenditure,

MXGP represents military spending as a percent of Gross Domestic Product (GDP) (mainly for postwar cases),

RV   stands for a revisionist power (refer to Table 1),

SQ   stands for a status quo power,

Δ indicates first differences figures $k_{t_1} - k_{t_0}$

$\Delta 2$ indicates differences as $k_{t_2} - k_{t_1}$

Measures using deflated military spending are labeled by the alphanumeric A1, A2 ... Ak while measures embodying deflated military spending as a proportion of GDP are labeled B1, B2 ... Bk. Since the meaning of military advantage in each operationalization is similar, both A and B measures are discussed together in this section. They are separated in the results and subsequent commentary since data on these measures derive from different but overlapping years.

Differences Indicators of Force Standing:

A1) MXSQ – MXRV*
    and   Direction of differences between rivals in expenditures in the same year.

A2) |MXSQ – MXRV| Absolute values of differences in expenditures in the same year.

A3) ΔMXSQ – ΔMXRV
    and   Directional differences and absolute values of differences between annual increments.

A4) |ΔMXSQ – ΔMXRV| (This measures *changing* force standing.)

B1) MXGPSQ – MXGPRV
    and   Directional differences, and absolute values of differences between racers' arming efforts proportional to their economies. (These measures may be more robust measures of true force standing, and of potential for protracted racing.)

B2) |MXGPSQ – MXGPRV|

B3) ΔMXGPSQ – ΔMXGPRV   Directional differences and absolute values of differences between annual increments

B4) |ΔMXGPSQ – ΔMXGPRV| in arming as a percent of GDP. (This taps economic potential as well as rates of change and presumably reflects the possibility of a quick alteration in relative

---

*The precedence of the status quo nation (always first) here is simply an ordering device which has no effect on the analyses. To guarantee that this theoretically expected result obtained, the author conducted two sets of analyses including one in which the revisionist power took precedence, and indeed the results were identical.

standing, as well as, more generally, a state's ability to carry on arms racing, to give up, or to go to war.)

Ratio Indicators of Force Standing:

Some writers and political decision makers consider various types of *ratio* indicators to be the best reflectors of relative military standing. (See Wallace, 1980, in which a "catch-up" ratio measuring the extent of the status quo power's decline or advance relative to the revisionist power is defined.) If ratio indicators best capture force standing as it operates to deter war, some of the following should help predict peace and war during periods when deterrence may be said to operate:

A5) $\dfrac{MXSQ}{MXRV}$

and

A6) $\dfrac{MXRV}{MXSQ}$

Since ratios 5 and 6 are not equal but inverse, both versions must be tested. Measure A6 is simply the ratio of the revisionist's arming to that of the status quo power, taking no account of prior arms stocks. Thus in the Soviet-American case, if the recent CIA Team report that the USSR might be "outspending" the U.S. by a factor of two were correct, B6 would show a value of two for that year and B5 would show a value of .5 for that year and that particular arms race, using the conventions adopted here. These measures may be said to focus on the country appearing in the numerator so that, as above, B6 shows the USSR "ahead" by a factor of 2, and B5 shows the U.S. "behind" by 50%.

B5) $\dfrac{MXGPSQ}{MXGPRV}$

and

B6) $\dfrac{MXGPRV}{MXGPSQ}$

A7) $\dfrac{\Delta MXSQ}{\Delta MXRV}$

and

A8) $\dfrac{\Delta MXRV}{\Delta MXSQ}$

Although much less complex, measure A7 appears to be crudely similar to that used by Wallace (1980) to predict crisis outcome. These measures are intended to capture relative rates of change in arming, assuming that nations arm—and go to war or not—basing their decisions on whether the relative size of increments in their armed forces is growing or shrinking. Measure A7 gives one possible interpretation of U.S. President Reagan's "margin of safety" for the U.S. against the USSR, a ratio of rates of change.

B7) $\dfrac{\Delta MXGPSQ}{\Delta MXGPRV}$

and

Possibly, increments in weapons levels relative to a rival would provide a more meaningful measure of deterrent ability if economic significance is also attached to the military measure, as in B7 and B8

B8) $\dfrac{\triangle\text{MXGPRV}}{\triangle\text{MXGPSQ}}$ in which annual arms increments as a proportion of GDP are used to measure relative military advantage.

Mixed Indicators of Force Standing:

These proposed measures make comparisons of the differences between rates of change in arms racing, catching up or falling behind, in two subsequent periods. Using these measures to predict deterrence success implies the more complicated argument that decisions about deterrence are not only influenced by relative increments in armed forces, or rates of change in relative increments, but by (perceived) changes over time in the increments' relative rates of change. That is, change in relative *speed* of racing may help predict deterrence success by, for example, "showing accelerating resolve," or by "demonstrating increasingly aggressive intentions."

A9) $\dfrac{\triangle 2\text{MXSQ}}{\triangle 2\text{MXRV}} - \dfrac{\triangle\text{MXSQ}}{\triangle\text{MXRV}}$

and

A10) $\dfrac{\triangle 2\text{MXRV}}{\triangle 2\text{MXSQ}} - \dfrac{\triangle\text{MXRV}}{\triangle\text{MXSQ}}$

B9) $\dfrac{\triangle 2\text{MXGPSQ}}{\triangle 2\text{MXGPRV}} - \dfrac{\triangle\text{MXGPSQ}}{\triangle\text{MXGPRV}}$

and

B10) $\dfrac{\triangle 2\text{MXGPRV}}{\triangle 2\text{MXGPSQ}} - \dfrac{\triangle\text{MXGPRV}}{\triangle\text{MXGPSQ}}$

These measures are suggested if relative advantage in rates of change in arming affects deterrence (a) if this effect is sensitive to perceived narrowing or widening of the gap between racers in relative rates of change, and/or (b) if this effect exists only relative to the economy. Two forms are advanced (one in absolute values: A11, A12; B11, B12).

A11) $\left| \dfrac{\triangle 2\text{MXSQ}}{\triangle 2\text{MXRV}} - \dfrac{\triangle\text{MXSQ}}{\triangle\text{MXRV}} \right|$

and

A12) $\left| \dfrac{\triangle 2\text{MXRV}}{\triangle 2\text{MXSQ}} - \dfrac{\triangle\text{MXRV}}{\triangle\text{MXSQ}} \right|$

B11) $\left| \dfrac{\triangle 2\text{MXGPSQ}}{\triangle 2\text{MXGPRV}} - \dfrac{\triangle\text{MXGPSQ}}{\triangle\text{MXGPRV}} \right|$

and

B12) $\left| \dfrac{\triangle 2\text{MXGPRV}}{\triangle 2\text{MXGPSQ}} - \dfrac{\triangle\text{MXGPSQ}}{\triangle\text{MXGPRV}} \right|$

Absolute values measures capture the (positive) distance between deterrers. Omitting absolute values gives some indication of whether "who is ahead" matters, since negative values may be introduced when differences are taken without absolute values.

CONTEXT OF TESTING: DETERRENCE

Each of the independent variables mentioned is used to measure military standing. While the literature does not appear to specify operationalizations, any of the four general deterrence hypotheses isolated from the literature could be confirmed or disconfirmed in these measures. If the appropriate configuration of any of the proffered force comparisons consistently deters, it should appear here as a good peace predictor *and* a good war predictor. For example, suppose the para bellum hypothesis, "status quo superiority implies peace" is true. If we test this proposition via force standing measure A5, arguing that deterrence success or failure is a function of the ratio $\frac{MXSQ}{MXRV}$, then cases in which the ratio exceeds one, showing a status quo advantage, should consistently be peace years and should be so classified. Years in which the ratio is less than one should consistently be years of deterrence failure and should be classified as war years. In either case there should exist a definite barrier at one. The discriminant analysis should use the hypothesized grouping—if it in fact exists in the data—to allow accurate prediction by finding the war group average ("centroid") well below one and the peace centroid well above one. This grouping would appear graphically illustrated in the accompanying histogram. (Note pun.)

Similar illustrations can be drawn for each general hypothesis in each operationalization of force standing, but constructing all possible results and their accompanying substantive interpretations would be excessively tedious. Instead, the results actually obtained will be presented, and those which show significant separations will be discussed. The consequences for the four general deterrence hypotheses can then be explored. Which power was generally "ahead" at the time war breaks out must be observed from the data for any relationships which are statistically significant.

METHOD OF ANALYSIS

Here the research problem is to predict a nominal dependent variable, war or peace, on the basis of comparisons between differences in force levels, to try to assess the usefulness of some general deterrence propositions. Ordinary Least Squares (OLS) techniques encounter several difficulties in this case since the dependent variable is dichotomous (Goldberger, 1964). Especially in the case that the dependent variable is drawn from a Bernoulli distribution, at least one OLS assumption is violated, in that the variance of the error term is then a function of the dependent variable (Cleary, 1980). In small samples, Generalized Least Squares (GLS) may be a more appropriate estimation technique than OLS (Theil, 1971) but even then, where the dependent variable is dichotomous, the functional form provided by GLS is "inherently unreasonable" (Cox, 1970; Cleary, 1980).

Discriminant analysis can be used to deal with dichotomous dependent variables in a more logical way. It appears that discriminant analysis was first developed by R. A. Fisher (1936) as a statistical instrument for classifying observations into two nonoverlapping groups[4] on the basis of the similarity of an observation to known members of the groups to be predicted. Here the attempt is to classify deterrence strategies as reflected in arming patterns in a given year, on the basis of each year's greater similarity either to the peace years or to the war years in the sample.

Discriminant analysis bears a limited analogy to regression analysis; the coefficients estimated can be shown to coincide under some sets of limiting assumptions (Cleary, 1980). However, there is a fundamental difference between the two procedures. While Linear Multiple Regression (LMR) estimates parameters for a model associating an additive linear combination of independent variables to minimize the squared error of the estimates of the dependent variable, discriminant analysis estimates coefficients so as to *maximize the differences* between dependent variable groups. In these analyses the technique is used to separate war and peace groups maximally.

This is done by choosing a computer program which maximizes the ratio of between-group sums of squares to within-groups sums of squares (Tatsuoka, 1971), using differential calculus to determine which weights on the independent variables will yield the greatest distinctions between war and peace groups.

It can be shown (Cleary, 1980:9-10) that the functions developed by discriminant analyses to predict group membership are directly tied to logistic functions (such as those used by Wallace, 1981) and that logistic functions can be derived from the discriminant functions.

This discussion has indicated that OLS methods are inappropriate for research problems such as the one at hand, in which the dependent variable is dichotomous. Since problems such as this one remain theoretically interesting and compelling in real life, a choice must be made among appropriate techniques, which include discriminant, logit and probit analyses.

Logit procedures may be preferable to discriminant analyses because the former make fewer assumptions. Logit, however, is unavailable to the author locally, and discriminant analyses have been shown to yield highly similar results (Gilbert, 1968). Halperin, Plackwelder and Verter (1971: 152) report that the significance of an independent variable (as indicated by the ratio of an estimated coefficient to the corresponding standard error) was "about the same" for analyses using both techniques on the same data. And in two studies of nonnormal research problems, Press and Wilson (1978) show that maximum likelihood estimates were only marginally superior to those obtained by discriminant function analysis.

In this first set of deterrence proposition tests, the potential but small differences in correct classifications which might appear under logit analysis did not seem to argue persuasively against the use of discriminant analysis, especially since results would be expected to parallel those of logit closely. This argues that discriminant function analysis is an informative technique for exploring the para bellum question, especially while deterrence hypotheses remain relatively ambiguous and relatively poorly specified. More detailed analyses following the introduction of greater precision in deterrence theorizing might require other methods.

The mean length of arms races examined here is about twelve years. Since there is some missing data, and since only annual defense budgets data exist for most of the arms races, this means an average maximum of 20-24 data points exists for each race, if we count two observations at each point in time, or 10-12 for indices. Consequently the races are too short to be confidently analyzed separately via techniques that assume a minimum sample size of approximately 30, and recent advances in small sample statistics have not changed this picture much. So, to increase sample size and to reflect the substantive arguments that deterrence is a general process at work over time and across nations, the present set of analyses is based on an aggregation of cases comprising years of arms racing, with each arms race treated as a subfile. The subfiles were created to prevent the introduction into the data of spurious information such as the differences between military expenditures in the final year of one race and the initial year of the next race with a new set of rivals. In each subfile one arms racer is labeled revisionist, the other status quo, with the exceptions noted in Table 3. Each military spending datum also carries a binomial code labeling it a war or peace year, to allow peace years to be analyzed separately. The aggregation then pools the military spending records for each arms race subfile but allows war and peace years to be contrasted, and allows status quo-challenger racing patterns to be separated. The aggregated data with these subdivisions allow some general observations to be made about the historical connection between prevalent force comparisons between rivals and political outcome. (See graphs of arms races in Appendix III.) (Some statistical problems may be produced by aggregation if error terms are correlated within subfiles.)

RESULTS

Here, if deterrence works, in any of the various comparative advantage or "catch-up" ratio forms indicated, the discriminant technique should be able to distinguish years of deterrence success (nonwar) from years of deterrence failure (war) strongly and significantly. On that basis the actual outcomes should correspond well to the predicted outcomes: there should be relatively few war years which are predicted as peace years, and conversely.

The first question that arises in interpretation of these results is whether any significant relationships have been uncovered. If the functions cannot distinguish significantly between war and peace years, the other aspects of the functions, including their classifications of each year into the predicted war or predicted peace category and their meaning for the deterrence hypotheses, are not of interest. Functions which do produce statistically significant separations[5] of war and peace years are then further described below to show their strength and the accuracy of the predictions they generate.

There are numerous indications of the statistical importance of predictions from discriminant function analyses. Here we focus on:

1) the statistical significance of outcome group separations;

2) the discriminating power of the function;

3) a measure of association between the outcome groups and the discriminant function;

4) interpretations of a classification matrix showing "hits" (correct classifications) and "misses" (incorrect group assignment).

If a significant separation of outcomes is not obtained initially, no further interpretation is called for. Here if deterrence success or failure could not be predicted at a significance level of .05 or better, the relevant discriminant function is presumed to be of little help in identifying force comparisons which deter.

However, especially if sample size is relatively large, high statistical significance does not necessarily imply the existence of strong relationships or of a large difference between outcome groups. To assess how well predicted the years of deterrence success and failure are, a measure of discriminating power is required. Contentionally, discriminating power is examined in two ways, via Wilks' lambda (λ) (Klecka, 1975:39) and via Tatsuoka's formulation of "discriminating power," which measures the total variability in the discriminant space attributable to group differences (Tatsuoka, 1970:48-49). Wilks' lambda (λ) is an inverse measure, whose values as they approach unity denote progressively less discrimination; values of lambda (λ) in the vicinity of zero show high group distinction. Tatsuoka's discriminating power measure indicates the degree of differentiation provided by the function, with higher values representing greater differentiation.

Another way to assess the strength of any relationships here is provided by the canonical correlation coefficient, r^*, whose values range from zero to one. The r^* reflects the degree of association between the outcome groups and the discriminant functions.

Strong significant results can also be shown graphically. In a stacked histogram for analyses of this sort, powerful separations are represented by clustering of one kind of cases at each extreme of the x axis, calibrated in outcome group centroid standard scores. (The deterrence success centroid, for illustration, is the peace group average and will be located, in the univariate case, at the most typical position on the x axis for the peace cases.) Weak results are indicated by a clustering of cases of both outcomes down the middle of the histogram more or less at zero, showing high similarity between years of deterrence success and failure. As is suggested by the selected histograms (pp. 65-66), most of the analyses conducted here show little group differentiation. This is also apparent in the classification matrices.

The classification matrix showing predictions generated by each function can be evaluated in several ways. In this context a perfect "hit-miss" table would look like this,

Actual Outcome	Predicted Outcome	
	Peace	War
Peace	100%	0%
War	0%	100%

with actual numbers of cases supplied, and with the strong upper left-lower right diagonal which you see here. Percentage of correct predictions can also be listed. In the tables of predicted outcomes an apparently substantively important proportion of correct predictions can be obtained in the problem at hand simply by predicting that all years are years of deterrence success—peace—because of the predominance of peace years in the sample. Since a theoretically useful model of deterrence must also be capable of predicting deterrence failure correctly, some correctly identified war years are of as much interest here as is a high rate of correct predictions overall. Again, persistently correct predictions are reflected in the outcome tables by strong diagonal elements and are summarized below the tables as "percent correctly classified."

Table 4 presents the results of twelve force comparisons used to predict deterrence success in two kinds of data, deflated military budgets and deflated military budgets as a percent of GDP, the latter largely confined to postwar cases. Because the sample size varies with the data, sample n is reported for each function. Statistical significance (α), measures of discriminating power, the canonical correlation, and the resulting classification matrix with percent correctly predicted are also shown. Histograms showing the greatest separations follow the table.

Note that two races had to be eliminated initially because military spending data were unavailable or extremely inaccurate, and because the foreign policies appear to be both revisionist in the Latin American case. These omitted races are the Chinese one with England and France in the 1860s and 1870s, and the Bolivian-Paraguayan competition in the 1920s and early 1930s. The Chinese-Japanese race is omitted because of the apparently inaccurate military spending figures for Japan. The early Russian-Japanese race is removed because of the difficulty in making a reasonable determination of revisionist or status quo foreign policies for the countries in question during the period.

There then remain partial data on twenty-eight races which cover 340 years inclusive. Because of several missing statistics, there are 329 data points as a maximum. Since GDP calculations are not generally available until after 1948, equations using this variable are only tested against postwar racing years, which gives a maximum n of 104.

57

TABLE 4
DISCRIMINANT FUNCTION RESULTS

Alpha-numeric	Measure	Wilk's L	F	x^2	S	Discriminating power	$r*$	Classification matrix
A1	MXSQ - MXRV n = 329	.99	4.82	4.78	.03	.01	.12	Predicted P W A P 305 10 c 96.8% 3.2% t u W 12 2 a 85.7% 14.3% l 93.31% correct
A2	|MXSQ - MXRV| n = 329	.99	4.51	4.47	.03	.01	.12	Predicted P W A P 305 10 c 96.8% 3.2% t u W 12 2 a 85.7% 14.3% l 93.31% correct
A3	dMXSQ - dMXRV n = 262	.99	.24	.24	.63	.00	.03	Predicted P W A P 14 235 c 5.6% 94.4% t u W 0 12 a 0% 100% l 9.92% correct
A4	|dMXSQ - dMXRV| n = 262	.99	.03	.03	.86	.00	.03	Predicted P W A P 8 242 c 3.2% 96.8% t u W 2 10 a 16.7% 83.3% l 6.87% correct
A5	MXSQ / MXRV n = 329	.94	19.16	18.59	.00	.05	.24	Predicted P W A P 305 10 c 96.8% 3.2% t u W 13 1 a 92.9% 7.1% l 93.01% correct

Alpha-numeric	Measure	Wilk's L	F	x^2	S	Discriminating power	r*	Classification matrix

A6 $\dfrac{MXRV}{MXSQ}$ n = 329

.99 2.23 2.22 .14 .004 .08

```
              Predicted
                P       W
A P   305      10
c    96.8%    3.2%
t
u W    12       2
a    85.7%   14.3%
l
     93.31% correct
```

A7 $\dfrac{dMXSQ}{dMXRV}$ n = 329

.92 22.20 21.30 .00 .07 .28

```
              Predicted
                P       W
A P   250       0
c    100%      0%
t
u W    11       1
a    91.7%    8.3%
l
     95.80% correct
```

A8 $\dfrac{dMXRV}{dMXSQ}$ n = 262

.99 .21 .21 .64 .00 .03

```
              Predicted
                P       W
A P    26     224
c    10.4%   89.6%
t
u W     1      11
a     8.3%   91.7%
l
     14.12% correct
```

A9 $\dfrac{d2MXSQ}{d2MXRV} - \dfrac{dMXSQ}{dMXRV}$ n = 220

.91 20.25 19.32 .00 .08 .29

```
              Predicted
                P       W
A P   209       0
c    100%      0%
t
u W    10       1
a    90.9%    9.1%
l
     95.45% correct
```

A10 $\dfrac{d2MXRV}{d2MXSQ} - \dfrac{dMXRV}{dMXSQ}$ n = 220

.99 .01 .01 .91 .00 .01

```
              Predicted
                P       W
A P   195      14
c    93.3%    6.7%
t
u W     9       2
a    81.8%   18.2%
l
     89.55% correct
```

Alpha-numeric	Measure	Wilk's L	F	x^2	S	Discriminating power	$r*$	Classification matrix

A11 $\left|\dfrac{d2MXSQ}{d2MXRV} - \dfrac{dMXSQ}{dMXRV}\right|$ n = 220 — .91   20.37   19.43   .00   .08   .29

```
          Predicted
            P       W
A  P  208        1
c     99.5%     .5%
t
u  W   10        1
a     90.9%    9.1%
l
     95.00% correct
```

A12 $\left|\dfrac{d2MXRV}{d2MXSQ} - \dfrac{dMXRV}{dMXSQ}\right|$ n = 220 — .99+   .07   .07   .79   .00   .02

```
          Predicted
            P       W
A  P   12      197
c     5.7%    94.3%
t
u  W    1       10
a     9.1%    90.9%
l
     10.00% correct
```

B1 MXGPSQ - MXGPRV   n = 103 — .95   5.45   5.28   .02   .04   .23

```
          Predicted
            P       W
A  P   81       17
c     82.7%    17.3%
t
u  W    3        2
a     60.0%    40.0%
l
     80.58% correct
```

B2 |MXGPSQ - MXGPRV| n = 103 — .96   4.50   4.38   .04   .03   .21

```
          Predicted
            P       W
A  P   82       16
c     83.7%    16.3%
t
u  W    4        1
a     80.0%    20.0%
l
     80.58% correct
```

B3 dMXGPSQ - dMXGPRV   n = 65 — .91   6.02   5.71   .02   .07   .30

```
          Predicted
            P       W
A  P   47       13
c     78.3%    21.7%
t
u  W    3        2
a     60.0%    40.0%
l
     75.38% correct
```

Alpha-numeric	Measure	Wilk's L	F	x^2	S	Discriminating power	r*	Classification matrix
B4	|dMXGPSQ - dMXGPRV|	.94	4.26	4.09	.04	.05	.25	Predicted

B4 |dMXGPSQ - dMXGPRV| .94   4.26   4.09   .04   .05   .25
    n = 65
```
                                                      Predicted
                                                       P      W
                                                 A P  49      11
                                                 c    81.7%   18.3%
                                                 t
                                                 u W   4       1
                                                 a    80.0%   20.0%
                                                 l
                                                     76.92% correct
```

B5 MXGPSQ   .99+   .44   .43   .51   .00   .07
    ‾‾‾‾‾‾
    MXGPRV
    n = 104
```
                                                      Predicted
                                                       P      W
                                                 A P  61      38
                                                 c    61.6%   38.4%
                                                 t
                                                 u W   2       3
                                                 a    40.0%   60.0%
                                                 l
                                                     61.54% correct
```

B6 MXGPRV   .99   .53   .53   .47   .00   .07
    ‾‾‾‾‾‾
    MXGPSQ
    n = 104
```
                                                      Predicted
                                                       P      W
                                                 A P  47      52
                                                 c    52.5%   52.5%
                                                 t
                                                 u W   2       3
                                                 a    40.0%   60.0%
                                                 l
                                                     48.08% correct
```

B7 dMXGPSQ   .98   1.22 1.19   .27   .003 .13
    ‾‾‾‾‾‾‾
    dMXGPRV
    n = 69
```
                                                      Predicted
                                                       P      W
                                                 A P  45      19
                                                 c    70.3%   29.7%
                                                 t
                                                 u W   2       3
                                                 a    40.0%   60.0%
                                                 l
                                                     69.57% correct
```

B8 dMXGPRV   .99   .10   .10   .75   .00   .04
    ‾‾‾‾‾‾‾
    dMXGPSQ
    n = 69
```
                                                      Predicted
                                                       P      W
                                                 A P  34      30
                                                 c    53.1%   46.9%
                                                 t
                                                 u W   1       4
                                                 a    20.0%   80.0%
                                                 l
                                                     55.07% correct
```

Alpha-numeric Measure	Wilk's L	F	x^2	S	Discriminating power	r*	Classification matrix

B9 d2MXG **PSQ** / d2MXG PRV — dMXGPSQ / dMX GPRV   .96   1.71   1.66   .20   .01   .20

n = 48

```
                 Predicted
                  P      W
         A  P    34     12
         c      73.9%  26.1%
         t
         u  W     1      1
         a      50.0%  50.0%
         l
              72.92% correct
```

B10 d2MXGPRV / d2MXGPSQ — dMXGPRV / dMXGPSQ   .99+   .05   .05   .82   .00   .03

n = 48

```
                 Predicted
                  P      W
         A  P    27     19
         c      58.7%  41.3%
         t
         u  W     1      1
         a      50.0%  50.0%
         l
              58.33% correct
```

B11 d2MXGPSQ / d2MXGPRV — dMXGPSQ / dMXGPRV   .99+   .04   .04   .85   .00   .03

n = 48

```
                 Predicted
                  P      W
         A  P    31     15
         c      67.4%  32.6%
         t
         u  W     1      1
         a      50.0%  50.0%
         l
              66.67% correct
```

B12 d2MXGPRV / d2MXGPSQ — dMXGPRV / dMXGPSQ   .97   1.19   1.16   .28   .004   .16

n = 48

```
                 Predicted
                  P      W
         A  P    20     26
         c      43.5%  56.5%
         t
         u  W     0      2
         a        0%   100%
         l
              45.83% correct
```

S represents statistical significance level

r* represents canonical correlation

d represents first difference terms

d2 represents (K_1-k_1) difference terms

DISCUSSION

Ten of the force comparison predictors drawn from the deterrence litera- ture yield functions significant at the .05 level or better. They are A_1, A_2, A_5, A_7, A_9, A_{11}, B_1, B_2, B_3, B_4. In both sets of data the relationships obtained using differences between current year military spending of rivals (A_1, A_2, B_1, B_2) were significant. Beyond these two shared features, the results diverge. Spending ratios were also significant deterrence success predictors in data set A (A_5), as were ratios of first differences (A_7 "catch- up" ratios) and differences between ratios of differences (A_9, A_{11}, rates of change in "catch-up" ratios), but only when status quo powers appeared in the numerator. These results suggest that ratio comparisons make some contribution to deterrence success but, as is shown below, it is a rather small contribution. The literature which calls for a status quo-challenger distinction would also appear supported here by the fact that ratio measures in which the revisionist appears in the numerator do not contribute to significant separations of war from peace years. That is, important relation- ships only emerge when this distinction is made and force standing is examined from the perspective of the status quo power.

In the GDP data, no ratio comparisons and none of the more complex differences measures were useful political outcome predictors. Differences between rates of arming as an economic effort (B_3, B_4), however, did allow significant prediction, emphasizing the dynamic aspect of the deterrence process, at least since 1948.

If another cutoff point besides significance level is introduced, r^* min- imum = .20, only the strongest relationships remain. They are A_5, A_7, A_9, A_{11}, and B_1, B_2, B_3, B_4. An r^* minimum of .20 is not, of course, a partic- ularly stringent requirement. In these analyses r^* never exceeds .30, and discriminating power never surpasses .09 (though the latter's possible range is .0 to 1.0). The equations discussed here produce significant but at best moderately weak results, exactly as would be expected if deterrence con- siderations were a real but relatively minor factor historically in the decision to go to war.

The force comparisons which fall into the more restrictive category, making significant though moderately weak contributions to explaining deterrence success/failure, are mostly (8/10) in the form "forces of country x – forces of country y." The overlapping category, ratio form, is represented four times (A_5, A_7, A_9, A_{11}), using rates of change and rough acceleration analogs. Evidently, in these data both general types of force comparison have some use in predicting political outcome, but the better predictors overall are the most dynamic ones (A_9, A_{11}), which use changes in ratios of first differences. Both A_9 and A_{11} show r*s among the strongest in these tests ($\cong$ .29), and discriminating power of .08, again representing a statistically significant but minor contribution to explaining deterrent success.

These discriminant analyses A_9 and A_{11}, however, while providing fair prediction of peace years, do not predict deterrence failure particularly effectively. Among the significant discriminant functions only the GDP data series B_1, B_2, B_3 and B_4 correctly classifies more than 15% of the deterrence failure years; two of these correctly identify 40% of the war cases (40% here is two cases out of five).

In this analysis the failure to predict war well is probably a reflection of a real lack of simple relationships at this level and is not an artifact of the technique's tendency to be unable to classify smaller group members correctly. As can be seen in the following selected histograms, few consistent group differences appear to exist. Observations on peace years are usually more varied among themselves than they are in comparison with war years on the measure examined here. This implies that none of these force comparisons has guaranteed deterrence success in the past, but instead that deterrence success occurs under a great variety of relative force standings, apparently dependent at least partially on factors omitted here (Doran, 1973; Lambeth, 1972).

An examination of the actual group means (see Table 5) for the stronger significant relationships can help illustrate this variety as well as to highlight the basic differences that appear to exist in the aggregate between years of deterrence success and failure.

In average terms, status quo powers appear to have predominated militarily over revisionist powers both in peace years as a group, and in the years during which interadversary war erupted, as a group. This is evidenced, for example, in the fact that measure A_5 (the ratio of status quo to revisionist military outlays) averages 18 in peace years (whereas it would average some number less than one if revisionists held superiority), and 301 in years deterrence fails. This status quo preponderance also appears at the individual nation level in some measures. In first differences, for example, status quo powers' increments are greater than those of their respective adversaries

GRAPHS:
SELECTED HISTOGRAMS

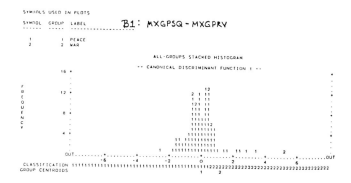

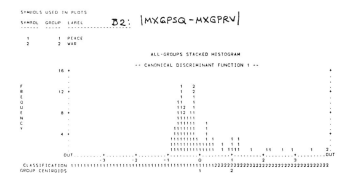

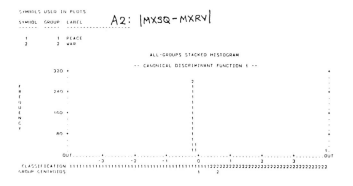

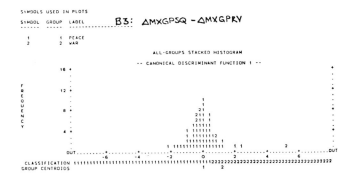

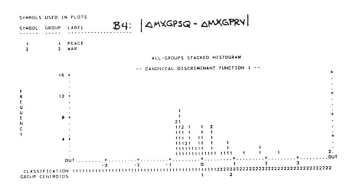

66

in 72% (13/18) of the final (war) year cases. Similarly, in the measure which shows the largest difference between peace and war years, A_9, the change in rates of change as ratios averages a small *negative* number during peacetime (-4). This would be expected in several circumstances; if, for example, status quo rates of arming were roughly constant and revisionist rates grew. For measure A_9, the war years averaged 3,086 (data have been transformed from dollar values to accommodate computer limitations), apparently reflecting a leap into war verified by graph inspection in these data and in other research (Alcock, 1972; Wallace, 1976:91-92; Wallace and Wilson, 1978:190-91; Smith, 1980) so that war years averaged over 771 times larger in absolute value on this measure than peace years. Even if direction of change in arming, a crucial point of information, is disregarded by taking absolute values for this measure (A_{11}), the tendency for peace years to show considerably smaller relative differences in arming rates of change is preserved. In none of the stronger significant relationships found here is this discrepancy between war and peace years *smaller* than two-to-one (B_2), with the already considered maximum (A_9) at 771.5. While the meaning of this general finding is not beyond debate, and causal links presumably travel through crisis and other proximal war cause variables, this observation does argue that in these rivalries, rapid acceleration in arming would be a poor war deterrer at this level of analysis.

TABLE 5
RATIOS OF ABSOLUTE VALUES OF WAR YEAR MEANS TO PEACE
YEAR MEANS FOR SELECTED FORCE COMPARIONS

		Ratio of war mean to peace mean
A5	$\dfrac{MXSQ}{MXRV}$	16.7
A7	$\dfrac{dMXSQ}{dMXRV}$	463.3
A9	$\dfrac{d2MXSQ}{d2MXRV} - \dfrac{dMXSQ}{dMXRV}$	771.5
A11	$\left\lvert \dfrac{d2MXSQ}{d2MXRV} - \dfrac{dMXSQ}{dMXRV} \right\rvert$	69.7
B1	MXGPSQ - MXGPRV	29.1
B2	$\lvert$ MXGPSQ - MXGPRV $\rvert$	2.0
B3	dMXGPSQ - dMXGPRV	27.1
B4	$\lvert$ dMXGPSQ - dMXGPRV $\rvert$	2.3

d represents first difference terms $(k_1 - k_0)$
d2 represents $(k_2 - k_1)$ difference terms

CONCLUSION: A LEAP INTO WAR?

Exponential growth in arming is a commonly observed pattern and has merited a central place in the literature. (See Appendix III; Richardson, 1960a; and many others.) However, in these data, arms competitions have taken a variety of forms, some with marked trigonometric tendencies in addition to exponential growth, and a few with logarithmic characteristics. (There is some indication that logarithmic arms races may be more likely to end pacifically than are races of other forms; because of small sample n, this possibility is conjectural.) Because arms racing is identified in current price figures but analyzed via deflated ones, because there exists the possibility of fluctuation about a pattern of growth, and because it is not excluded definitionally, some eight final arms racing years before wars here show a negative increment, although at high absolute levels of arming. This is generally a drop away from a maximum in the prior (penultimate) year and so should not be seen necessarily as evidence against the existence of a historically noted gathering of forces into the final part of arms racing, signalling deterrence failure, especially since figures in Table 5 would show even greater contrast if these cases were omitted. In the present data set, for races with revisionist or status quo foreign policy designations, about 71% (24/34) of the war-ended national cases show a positive final increment. Of these increments, 83% (20/24) are larger than the average increment within each race during years of deterrence success. In fact, they are considerably larger. The mean ratio of war years' positive increments to average increments within races during years of deterrence success is 56.44. That is, on the average, deterrence failure years' increments, when they are positive, are about 56 times larger than the average increase prevailing within war-ended rivalries. Final years' increments for rivalries settled without war, when they are positive (.67 or 4/6), also are on the average larger than the prevailing increments, but this difference is much less pronounced, amounting to a factor of about 4.1. This difference between war and peace increments argues that there is something peculiar about years of deterrence failure even in the restricted context of each local bilateral competition; they are characterized on the average by unusually large spurts in arming, though some cases of decreases do exist. This sudden expansion before war has been argued or documented in other sources for arms racing in general (Huntington, 1958; Wallace, 1972) and for the pre-World War I and interwar cases in particular (Wallace, 1976:91).

This leap into war can be seen, albeit somewhat less clearly, in the slight preponderance of positive second derivatives (acceleration indicators) during years of deterrence failure. For the total sample of racing nations irrespective of foreign policy, when a race lasts at least ten years to allow curve-fitting, 61% of the cases show positive second derivatives in the year deterrence fails. In these data the meaning of this observation is somewhat problematical since all the peace outcome years for longer races ($n > 10$) show positive second derivatives as well. Apparently the absolute level of arming and the atypical size of final increments (56x as opposed to 4x) distinguish war from peace years here.

There is some preliminary indication here that deterrence failure may be signalled by negative *third* derivatives in racing; when rates of change in acceleration flag, a special risk may exist (Alcock, 1972). The Cuban Missile Crisis marks one such year for the U.S. in these data.

There is also some evidence here that among the longer arms races (ten years or more), wars tend to follow rivalries which, when plotted, are concave up with some exponential component, while other settlements follow races which are largely concave down, whether they are of logarithmic or other form. This can be seen by inspection of the plotted data and is verified when curves are fit. (See Appendix III.)

So there apparently exists immediately before deterrence fails a material surge in arming in some measures, evidently dominated by the status quo powers in average terms. In seven of eight significant but at best moderate relationships (88%, including A_5, A_9, A_{11}, B_1, B_2, B_3 and B_4), war year means are large and positive, favoring the status quo countries. Omitting the relationships A_{11}, B_2 and B_4 because of their close similarities to others, the war year averages remain large and positive for 80% (4/5) of the significant relationships without absolute value terms.

Conversely, for ended races, in most instances (13/20, or 65% of all cases; 12/17, or 71% of war-ended cases; 1/3, or 33% of peace-ended cases) revisionists' average increments *within* races exceed those of status quo powers during the competition and excluding the last year for which records exist, whether this is a war year or not. Exceptions include the Finnish/ Soviet case and the first Indian/Pakistani case. In the whole sample of ended races regardless of outcome, omitting the outcome year data, revisionists' increments average about 870 times status quo powers' increments before deterrence fails. This overwhelmingly large ratio stems from the relatively low starting points of some revisionist racers, and from the predominance of pre-World War II Germany in these figures. When the German cases are excluded as outliers, the status quo powers on the average appear marginally ahead in aggregate terms (average increments) thoughout arms racing, by a factor of approximately 1.59. Interestingly, this margin is somewhat larger in peacefully terminated races alone (1.87), but it is unclear that this constitutes a significant difference.

There appears here some evidence for a status quo edge in final arms rivalry years, whether this final year is a war year or a peace year. Ostensibly, there is some resolution of disputes in the offing when status quo powers take the upper hand unambiguously; whether it is a war or nonwar outcome seems to be associated with the magnitude of the effort.

CONCLUSION: SUPPORT FOR
DETERRENCE HYPOTHESES

Relative force level comparisons make a consistently small but significant contribution to explaining deterrence failure between rivals whose mutual disputes and foreign policy attitudes could be used in these data to categorize revisionist and status quo powers. Data to test the hypothesized deterrence relationships reveal considerable variety in arming patterns across time and nations, yet some general features of relative force standing consistently help predict political outcome. The strongest findings here are:

1) Ratio measures of different kinds are sensitive to deterrence success and failure;

2) War years appear to be signalled by greater disparity between rivals than was prevalent earlier;

3) Major changes in arming in the status quo powers' favor, marked by positive second derivatives in some cases, are associated with an end to the rivalry, with larger increments preceding war and relatively smaller ones preceding other settlements;

4) There may exist a special risk of war in the vicinity of decreases after local maxima in arming, perhaps because of the new uncertainty thus induced in international perceptions of threat;

5) Either deterrence functions differently when measured via arming as an economic effort, or deterrence functions somewhat differently since 1948;

6) Most but not all arms racing eventually ends in war.

The first findings have already been discussed at some length, and their meaning for the deterrence hypotheses which were set forth in an earlier section is discussed below. (See also Table 6.) The last finding deserves some comment. At the most generous possible assessment, four of twenty-five terminated races (16%) have ended in some way other than war. These cases presumably would not exist if arms racing were simply war by another

TABLE 6
RESULTS FOR SPECIFIC HYPOTHESES

Hypothesis precis:	Results
H_1 Deterrence works while status quo power leads.	Confirmed in relatively slow arms racing Disconfirmed in rapid acceleration (As expected in exponential processes)
H_2 Equality promotes peace.	Fairly general confirmation
H_3 Equality promotes war.	Generally disconfirmed, with some exceptions
H_4 Deterrence works while revisionist power leads.	Less well-confirmed than H_1 for slow slow racing. When Germany is included, some weak case-specific confirmation. Possible confirmation in rapid racing.

name.[6] They include (1) Norway/Sweden; (2) Russia/Japan (if dropping a race to resume it and fight later is admissible as a nonwar outcome); (3) Iran/Iraq (brief rapprochement before war); (4) Indonesia/Malaysia.

That at a minimum 84% of these involvements ended in war suggests that for whatever reasons (arms racing dynamics, threat perceptions, crisis escalation, boredom, accident, prospects of substantial gains, or a congeries of other variables—notably alliance factors), there is a powerful tendency for deterrence to fail over time across many nations. This failure may be expected for several reasons (see especially Deutsch, 1968), including but not limited to:

1) All social growth in systems perceived to be closed may be inherently conflictful (Choucri and North, 1975); alternatively, all armaments outside law may be inherently provocative (Waskov in Kissinger, ed., 1965:78);

2) Economic bounds on arms buildups may exist (Caspary, 1967) and war pressures may rise at the boundaries (Choucri and North, 1975);

3) Even initially utterly credible threats may decay over time through lack of use, and at both ends of the spectrum of value of objectives. There is some empirical evidence (Doran, 1973) that credibility declines rapidly as the value of the objective diminishes. Thus Weede (1976:410) finds that "overwhelming preponderance" (an advantage of 10/1 or more) "is more effective in preventing major rather than minor military conflicts. . . ." (Incredibility of threat is also generated when threat magnitude is out of proportion to the objective; hence the incredibility of mutual assured destruction.) Similarly, credibility of threat against actions to achieve maximally valued objectives becomes irrelevant;

4) Crazy states (Cambodia/Kampuchea under Pol Pot) or crazy leaders may emerge (Dror, 1971), and may be both threatening and undeterrable. Similarly, entire classes of objectives may be so highly prized that efforts to attain them are undeterrable ("secure" borders, aspiring-nationalist guerrilla war);

5) Human choice may not really approximate decision making processes which follow formal axioms about utility maximization (Ellsberg, 1961), especially in crisis. That is, deterrence only works when you do not need it;

6) Cumulative probability of successful sequential crisis management may approach zero over time (Deutsch, 1968);

7) Technological bounds on racing may not exist; proliferation of entities raises prospects of deterrence failure by technical accident;

8) Rapid introduction of new weapons systems may raise incentives for preempting (deterrence instability);

9) Some racing patterns may tend at a deterministic level to increase without bounds, or without bounds that are temporally meaningful to humans (Smith, 1980). In these patterns showing mathematical instability, deterrence may fail because of high risk, high threat perceptions, or public fatigue;

10) Deterrence may not be about war prevention.

The assessment of these results must be made cautiously within the limitations imposed by the fact that none of the canonical r's exceeds .30. Insofar as the discriminant evidence was significant but not particularly strong, raw data, curve-fitting and graph observations have been incorporated for clarity into the interpretations of the results.

There is here some qualified support for the view that parity is related to deterrence success (H_2), since years of peace in military competition have been characterized by much smaller differences between adversaries' force ratios generally than are years of deterrence failure. The moderately successful relationships which are found here capitalize (note pun) on this difference. Notwithstanding, this finding does not necessarily imply that arms control efforts aimed at real or paper parity will, if they achieve their goals, reduce war risks in individual cases, because in many specific instances peace years are widely scattered on all measures examined while some—though not many—arms race-related wars have begun when annual arming levels were close (France/Germany) or when increments were virtually identical. This scattering of years of deterrence success on several measures implies that force matching is not necessarily a peace correlate in any particular rivalry. (See also Rummel, 1976:55, in which arms control, without accompanying political changes, is not associated with bilateral peace.) At the same time, there are so few cases of rivals who were roughly equal at the point deterrence failed that H_3 cannot be supported. The view that rough equality promotes war is disconfirmed in the discriminant function analyses by the same evidence which supports the opposite view H_2, that equality may be peace related.

There is some sporadic and highly preliminary support for the view that an average edge in *increments* for the revisionist correlates with deterrence success. However, this observation is reversed if the pre-World War II German rivalries, which are statistically extreme, are removed from the analyses. (Normalization via logged values is impractical here since a few very small numbers are included in the data set; while bringing in the outliers, logged values obscured most of the variance.)

Finally, there is rather more support for the view that abrupt positive changes (and some abrupt negative changes) in arming may be war related, especially if the former are quite large. Status quo powers have tended to

76

hold an edge throughout racing in some measures, and this preponderance is, on the average, substantially greater in the crisis year as war begins than it is in peacetime, or in peaceful solutions following crises. Great increases in status quo superiority appear to be war related, whether in and of themselves or because of some complex intervening processes. This appearance argues against the status quo para bellum hypothesis (H_1), except that the relationship may be due to arguably arbitrary choices of status quo-revisionist power designations. Some literature maintains that this designation is immaterial; it is the abrupt change in arming itself which may be destabilizing in either or both the deterrence or mathematical sense(s) (Richardson, 1960a); and which may be tied to crises (Choucri and North, 1975), hence to war (Holsti, 1972). If this assertion is true, the theoretical significance of the associated finding lies in the magnitude of the differences between arming in years of deterrence failure as opposed to arming in years of deterrence success.

However that may be, the relationships on which these observations are based, though significant, do not account for enough of the variance in political outcome to preclude the possibility that other omitted variables are equally important. Case studies are required to focus parity-superiority questions at the individual nation level to yield more detailed, data point-by-point results. Further theoretical development, in which initial conditions of deterrence propositions are specified, is also necessary (George and Smoke, 1974).

CONCLUSION: IMPLICATIONS FOR DETERRENCE THEORIZING

This research is relevant to interrival wars originating in short-term provocative events or crises, rather than to the potential for war among arms racers which might begin slowly in an unorthodox way. As an example of an application to which this research would be irrelevant, an unorthodox war origins scenario can be provided for the U.S. and USSR: through gradual escalation from protracted conventional theater engagements in Europe or the Third World, the superpowers are drawn into a spiral of incremental commitments to opposing contingents, at last facing one another.

Some studies (Quandt, 1976) suggest that such unorthodox scenarios are in fact improbable since one or both superpowers could be expected on the basis of their prior historical records to move quickly to minimize the results of a superpower confrontation. This minimization was apparently the Soviet response to the October 1973 Middle East War, a recent crisis with great escalation potential, and some authors argue that conservative, risk-containing crisis responses are typical of the Soviets (Triska, 1968:346). Arguably, this is a mutual response in most U.S.-USSR confrontations (Coffey, 1971:37); however, the exceptions are dramatic enough to retain the possibility for consideration (e.g., the Cuban Missile Crisis).

In these data the results obtained are probably most applicable to deterrence of direct attack on the nation, for several reasons, including the incorporation of this idea in the definition of deterrence failure. Because the sample of final race years is too small to be divided by category of proximal war (or peace) cause, no systematic determination of the applicability of these results to deterrence of lesser but still extremely provocative events or of moderately provocative events could be made. The literature suggests that results such as these are probably not very relevant to the last type of deterrence, and possibly that such events in this category are not readily deterrable.

SUMMARY

There are two basic conjectures, with several variants, at issue here. One is that foreign policy attitude toward a rival nation (revisionist or status quo) affects deterrence success. The other is that some straightforward comparisons of force ratios called for in the literature predict deterrence success. If the first proposition holds, those measures which make a distinction between revisionist and status quo powers should generate better predictions than analyses which ignore this difference. If the second proposition holds, at least some of the force ratio functions should predict political outcome accurately, depending on the operationalizations employed.

Here foreign policy designations *do* affect deterrence success, though in a way counter-intuitive to American analysts. An initial set of analyses not incorporating foreign policy attitude yielded uniformly dismal predictors. When status quo-revisionist distinctions are used, some significant results are obtained. Ratio measures which focused on the revisionist (revisionist in the numerator) were never good predictors; the race seems to be to the status quo power, in more ways than one.

In the whole sample, the most dynamic formulations (A_9, A_{11}), those approximating changes in ratios of first differences in arms, contributed the best predictors. In contrast, in the smaller GDP data set ratio measures were usually not useful (B_9 is an exception) and the apparently less informative differences measures predominated. This suggests either of two counter-intuitive prospects: one, that just when some analysts considered deterrence the most "delicate," it was least sensitive to change (post-1948); or two, that while deterrence failure is sensitive to rates of change in arming, the economic effort that arming represents is superfluous or even confounding information in ratio form. This might be expected if Caspary (1967) is correct that economic constraints do not exert much effect on arms accumulation, and that the boundaries economic limits may impose are (at least theoretically) rather distant. This prospect is relevant to the deterrence failure question if we assume that at the economic boundaries,

81

pressures to preempt (or capitulate, or declare victory and do nothing more) rise and/or public pressures for a more (or less) aggressive foreign policy grow.

United States strategic weapons planning and disarmament proposals have at their base fundamentally untestable assumptions about intentions and values of Soviet, Chinese and other decision makers (White, 1969). These assumptions are necessary and may be more or less useful. However, to avoid casting an aura of specious scientific validity about decisions in these spheres, it is necessary to ferret out such assumptions and to realize that a case may be made for any policy in any country in deterrence-theoretical terms. This ambiguity points to the need for a more rigorous and formal general theory of deterrence, and for empirical tests of potentially law-like relationships, including case study applications.

The present analysis shows that force ratio comparisons, while significant predictors, explain relatively little about the outbreak of war following periods of military rivalry. The existence of the race itself seems to provide a powerful force making for war, a conjecture which is given more rigorous confirmation in comparisons of the predictive value of arms race indices as opposed to deterrence indices (Wallace, 1980; 1981).

This research implies that while deterrence considerations have made a significant contribution historically to the decision to go to war, they are not determining factors but may be outweighed by other considerations, especially including calculated changes in foreign policy (Rummel, 1976). The results summarized above also suggest that status quo powers may not be perpetually relied upon to guard the peace, although they may enjoy a unique responsibility for so doing, and that Waskov (in Kissinger, 1965:77) may be right in asserting that short-run deterrence stability leads to long-run deterrence instability, increasing the chances for war over time.

Perhaps many real deterrence relations are substantially more complex than the ones tested, but some rather complex indices have been developed here. The speculation of insufficient complexity, especially in view of the generally poorly specified antecedent conditions accompanying deterrence propositions in much of the literature, does not provide sufficient grounds to begin aggregated empirical testing at points of greater detail. (However, the war variable itself might profitably be operationalized in a more complex nonnominal way.)

By shearing away many culturally relative questions, the nature of underlying disputes and other historical factors, perceptual issues, psychological war propensity and variations in tactics and strategy, this analysis presents in some ways the simplest possible general quantitative assessment of fundamental deterrence propositions. The fact that the results obtained here echo Wallace's findings (1981) in a different data set via contrasting methods further supports the contention that marked status quo superiority *in se* is not a reliable safeguard of peace between arms race rivals.

This research suggests that an increase in the size of increments in arms racing characterizes final years; whether it is a war or peace year appears to depend in part on the size of the increment. Relatively large changes in racing such as those enacted and proposed for fiscal 1983 by the Reagan administration in the U.S. may theoretically be associated with the resolution of some outstanding issues under contention, as could be predicted via a submissiveness model (Richardson, 1960a). Thus it may be a propitious time to discuss the nuclear status of Europe, or the future direction of intercontinental arming. It is tempting to accept the bargaining suggestion that concessions are more forthcoming to a state which negotiates from a superior position; however, this conclusion does not seem to be forthcoming from the empirical bargaining literature (Hopmann, 1972; Zartman, ed., 1978). (Even the analogy of "bargaining chips" is flawed, since a chip is used to bluff with, not to deploy.) In the arms control example, there have been so few truly significant concessions that it would be difficult to assess this contention on the basis of the evidence of ratified concessions.

It is similarly difficult to see this type of substantial positive change in U.S. racing associated with major Soviet concessions in strategic armament research and development in the next several years, given the investment of both sides in technologies for interceptor-destructor satellites, antisubmarine warfare, enriched particle beam weapons, etc. Thus we are left with the prospect that it may be a risky interlude.[7]

If arms racing in these data has not served a consistent deterrent function, then perhaps its defense value should be emphasized. Snyder makes this distinction:

> . . . deterrence means discouraging the enemy from taking military action by posing for him a prospect of cost and risk outweighing his prospective gain. Defense means reducing our own prospective costs and risks in the event that deterrence fails (Snyder, 1961:3).

It is in this sense that arms racing may be understood not as war prevention—deterrence of aggression against the racer (though not necessarily *by* the racer)—but as a tactic for national preservation or defense, even though it may heighten the prospects of war should deterrence fail.

The defense function should be examined more rigorously because arms racing appears not to prevent war. If it did, substantially more races should have ended nonviolently. Racing may reduce the incidence of war in some cases, but this is in principle an assertion which cannot be directly tested.

If racing does not minimize the risk of aggressive war on or by the arms racer, conceptualizing arms racing as a survival guarantee, the so-called insurance factor of arming, is still reasonable, at least prior to the advent of nuclear weapons. This is so because although historically arms racers often became entangled in wars, few were destroyed as national entities in these wars, as presumably they might have been had they possessed no substantial military capabilities. Horizontal and vertical nuclear proliferation may change this prospect.

It is often argued as a matter of policy that in an uncertain world, a bit of overpreparation in military matters is far more desirable than under-preparation in any amount. There is little support for that view here if war prevention is the primary goal. Even the defense rationale of arms racing is unclear, since if one compares casualties of arms race-related war with those of nonarms race-related war, using Correlates of War data to identify the wars and provide the casualty counts, wars preceded by arms racing have on the average taken considerably more lives.[8]

FOOTNOTES

1. (Note pun.) The exception to this exclusion occurs in the case, trivial at this point and apparently untrue, that all arms competition is seen as risking war.

2. This deflator from the U.S. Department of Commerce is based on the proportion of Gross National Product (GNP) which federal government purchases of goods and services comprise in a given year. It appears in *The National Income and Product Accounts* for the U.S. with 1972 = 100. It is argued that this federal purchases deflator is more appropriate for application to military spending than is a consumer price index since some elements of defense purchases are not priced in the civil sector and may be subject to rather different economic pressures. Post hoc it appeared that this government purchases index bears considerable similarity to the consumer price index for the same period. Indices for the USSR and the People's Republic of China (PRC) were obtained from correspondence with SIPRI economist Richard Booth.

3. Scholars who wish to draw powerful conclusions from simplifying assumptions in their arguments occasionally allege that the truth or falsity of axioms in an argument is immaterial. However, this contention is false. In a deductive argument, falsity of axioms is always propagated in the conclusion(s), and in an inductive argument, falsity may appear.

4. Discriminant analysis is well established in fields such as education and psychology, where it is used to predict educational and occupational success (Weiss, 1973). In political science, discriminant analyses have been applied to voting behavior (Klecka, 1973) and to the disposition of felony cases (Eisenstein and Jacob, 1977), for example. Klecka (1980) gives other actual or imagined applications including a hypothetical prediction of safe release of hostages based on a congeries of variables such as n of captors and n of weapons at hand.

5. It should be acknowledged that significance tests strictly speaking apply only to procedures on probability samples. Since in this research design a random sample was not feasible due to the tiny sample n which would inevitably result from drawing from a parent population of arms races whose members through 1977 number only 32, the assumptions of significance tests are not necessarily strictly met. (Of course, random

samples of years within races could be taken, but in this analysis no information was discarded as random sampling would have required.) Klecka (1975:38) suggests that when probability samples are unavailable, the best option is to "interpret test results conservatively" and to rely more heavily on the possible substantive importance of the results.

6. Arms racing and war may be directed toward the same objectives, such as recovering disputed territory or reestablishing a secure border. Then if racing achieves the objective, war is unnecessary. This merely emphasizes the differences between the two as implements of foreign policy. (War and arms competition also serve somewhat different domestic functions.) Note that wars often begin without arms racing (about half the Correlates of War inter-state wars were not arms race related, including for example the Franco-Prussian, Spanish-American and Korean wars) and arms racing may end without war (Malaysia/Indonesia), neither of which would necessarily be expected if arms rivalries were simply a deterministic war prelude.

7. There is a nonzero risk of an ecological fallacy in applying the results of aggregate analyses to particular cases, as is done to some degree here in the interpretation of the U.S.-Soviet military relationship. This risk is mitigated to the extent that the aggregate analyses have been supplemented with other case-specific information which supports the discussion at the dyad level.

8. Differences between mean total battle deaths for race-related as opposed to other international wars $\cong 1,293,695$; $\alpha \cong .10$. When outliers (the two world wars and the Korean War) are removed, a difference still exists but it is smaller and less significant: difference in means $\cong 11.2$; $\alpha \cong .20$. At the aggregate level this argues against the hypothesized loss-minimizing function of arms racing, if we assume population is the variable whose loss is minimized.

APPENDIXES

APPENDIX I
A Variety of Reasons for Relatively Weak Results

Myriad explanations exist for the lack of successful deterrence relations besides the ever present possibility that, as some authors argue (Rummel, 1976), no such general relationship can exist. The paucity of deterrence relationships uncovered here may be due to the simplicity of associations suggested, although this parsimony has a base in the literature. For further investigation, a variety of considerations which enhance the complexity of hypothesized deterrence functions may make such functions more realistic, hence more accurate, predictors.

1) Form of model incorrectly specified

Possibly, time should be treated differently in these analyses. More dynamic models might be required. Time lags allowing for perception and contemplation of rivals' arsenals might be advantageous. Interactive terms may be required.

A more disconcerting possibility is that discontinuities in the deterrence process may exist at several junctures, so that the assumption of continuity over the span of arms racing may be an awkward and inaccurate one. Step-level changes of several kinds may be imagined. For some rivals, a nuclear overkill capability could mark a discontinuity. Radical alterations in destructive capacity or in effective defense generally, denoting level-of-magnitude changes, could mark discontinuities in deterrence thinking. These discontinuities could be expected at points where a locally "ultimate" weapon such as the cross-bow, gunpowder, or repeating rifles are developed; or where a locally impervious defense such as armored fighting ships or a laser anti-ballistic missile (ABM) first emerges. Discontinuities might also exist if the number of alliances or strength of allies is greatly changed, because of the partial substitutability of reliable allies and national military preparations. A change of national political leadership might even produce discontinuities in the proposed deterrence process because of the

89

introduction of new and different decision makers' subjective perceptions. War prevention results might also be muddied if deterrence itself, or some relevant but unmeasured deterrence component such as credibility, operates in a way which is strongly and persistently nonlinear over time, either evidencing strong fluctuations, rapid growth or decline or some other features showing a precise form. Suppose, for example, that over some threshold, credibility of threat gradually diminishes over time (Etzioni, 1964:183), ceteris paribus, and that this diminution is speeded up by diffusion of comparable weapons technology, sequential crisis survival, etc., so that even while arsenals grow, credibility might remain constant (or even decline). Credibility could then be a logarithmic function of time whose contribution to deterrence success initially grows rapidly but then levels off. (Logarithmic relations are documented in the social sciences. See, for instance, Midlarsky [1974:429] in which n of alliances and polarity are positively logarithmicly related to likelihood of war outbreak.) Such complications could obscure any relationships which might exist in these data.

2) Statistical clues

Potentially logit analysis could yield more robust results than those obtained here with discriminants. However, this eventuality is unlikely since the technique employed is the more generous of the two and the one more probably capable of estimating significant coefficients where, arguably, none operate (Halperin, Plackwelder and Verter, 1971:152). Probabilistic techniques might be advanced.

Another possible difficulty could be the existence of an unknown intervening variable through which deterrence may have effect. A more formal theory of deterrence would clarify this issue.

3) Incorrectly specified variables

Professional military analysts and others hold that specific force ratios have little to do with deterrence, but that a better predictor would be best-guess estimates of *surviving* forces, judged on the basis of the probable results of an encounter between one rival's offensive forces and the defensive systems of the attacked nation (Lowe, 1964:197). Surviving forces' destructiveness then would be determined as some weighted combination of accuracy, detonating power, target hardening or other factors appropriate to the geography and technology. Presumably, where effective defenses do not exist, as against ballistic missile nuclear bombardment, the attacker's loss to defensive systems goes to zero and simple force comparisons corrected for malfunctions again become relevant. The importance of the loss-to-defense quantity in deterrence thinking may then have diminished since 1945 at least for nuclear-armed or nuclear-targeted rivals, but its omission still could have had a role in confounding the statistical results presented above. However, if this quantity must be included, deterrence theorizing for rivals which have not recently been belligerents (and hence have no well-grounded estimates of probable loss-to-defense under some circumstances) is further removed from general empirical test since cross-national defense loss estimates will be conjectural and potentially highly variable over time, geography, weapons and command-and-control systems. Further complicating this difficulty is the possibility that some idiosyncratically weighted combination of adversaries' projections and perceptions of surviving forces forms the actual deterrent. Perceptual data also prove elusive, a difficulty which is compounded across nations and major linguistic groups.

Some authors suggest that *cumulative* force levels are the actual deterrents. If this is so, use of annual measures in these analyses may account for the weak results. Cumulative force levels present some measurement difficulty since, first, we do not know when to start cumulating. Secondly, if budget measures of arsenals are admissible, they must be discounted by some unknown, variable and probably idiosyncratic factors to reflect force erosion and replacement over time, varying across wide ranges of climate, terrain, and use and maintenance practices.

Another possibility is that greater complexity in the annual data is required. Index construction (Wallace, 1979) may be recommended.

4) Variables omitted but knowable

The literature proffers a rich range of variables which could be included in these analyses. As Goldhamer notes for the Soviet case:

> An examination of the historical record suggests that the degree of Soviet aggressiveness to be deterred is a function not only of the strategic balance but also of certain preferred political strategies, the experience of special failures, the style and character of particular leaders, and Soviet emphasis on political warfare. The strategic balance has had to vie with these and other influences (Goldhamer, 1971:5).

Some of these and other advocated deterrence-relevant variables are measurable, at least at the nominal and ordinal levels. Some factors (such as Turner's "mendacity coefficient" and Goldhamer's defense by bluff) could be given rough estimates today by comparison of some classes of claims with aerial surveillance evidence.

5) Variables omitted but essentially unknowable

Other reasons for the general failure to observe strong deterrence relations here may lie in the possibility that crucial variables, while they have some—possibly determining—effect, are not empirical. That is, Ellsberg (1968) may be right when he says there may be no logical solution to the deterrence question; deterrence may be an art. If deterrence is an art, there can be no expectation that its study should yield testable propositions.

The case for deterrence as Zen, as an artistic discipline, rests on the profoundly subjective nature of assessments (such as Snyder's [1961] in the classic *Deterrence and Defense*) of adversaries' intentions, values of objectives, probabilities of attaining them, likelihood of retaliation, expected severity of retaliation under given defenses, etc. As Singer elaborates:

> Obviously, no two individuals will combine them [such dimensions] in the same fashion, give the same weight to the variables that affect success or failure, or attach the same importance [consciously or otherwise] to each dimension. . . . these factors may hardly be considered at all by either the careless or the irrational (Singer, 1962:25).

6) The assumption of perfect (or at least reasonably good) information

Imperfect information could also disrupt relationships which might otherwise exist between (known) force comparisons and deterrence failure. Arguably this is a diminishing problem over time as communications technology flourishes. However, for the effects of information problems to diminish simply because of proliferation of communications means, effective *secrecy* must be roughly constant, opportunities for decision makers to communicate must at least stay the same, "disinformation" must have little effect, and no one must be playing defense (or deterrence) by bluff, at least successfully. It is unclear that these conditions hold generally. While lack of perfect information may have some effects, probably lagging the relationships (but also possibly altering military procurement), the direction of change in information supply is unobvious, and required time lags or induced over- or underreactions appear case-specific and highly idiosyncratic.

7) Deterrence as war timing

Another explanation for the dearth of relationships here may stem from the possibility that deterrence is not designed to preclude the war option but to maneuver it over time. If advantageous force ratios were not planned in most of these arms rivalries to *prevent* rival-to-rival war, but only to raise the odds of prevailing in a crisis, or to affect the *timing* of eventual war, there would be no necessary relationship between postulated force levels and the onset of war (Lider, 1977:346-48).

8) Deterrence and Compellance

Schelling's conceptual distinction between deterrence (dissuading an adversary) and compellance (imposing one's own will) is not made here, and could confound results if these terms only rarely coincide in practice. While in particular cases the two terms' referents could of course coincide, this coincidence is not strictly necessary, especially if compellance refers to coercing rivals into hitherto uncontemplated acts. This distinction might be made in future analyses (Schelling, 1966: esp. chapter 2). It is possible (but not necessary) that in many cases these are symmetrical terms: "they" try to deter what "we" try to compel, and conversely. Not all issues will necessarily be polarized in this way, as rivals may have common interests. Hence, two powers might combine forces to "compel" a third party, etc.

9) Status quo or not: other readings of history

The designations of adversaries' foreign policies as fundamentally status quo or revisionist are made only with respect to that sector of foreign policy directed toward the rival. Thus the same country may at the same time appear revisionist in its policies toward one rival, and status quo toward another. However, any such designations may be debatable. Obviously, divergence from these foreign policy categorizations could potentially have great effect on the results.

Many developments can be imagined which might better specify deterrence propositions; however, a number of them militate against testability. A more rigorous formal theory of deterrence is called for, which could set closure conditions and incorporate all required variables including those which may be potentially impossible to operationalize (Hempel, 1965). Such a theory and its consequences could guide future research, and indicate which caveats have some bearing on these results.

10) The arms racing cases

It has been pointed out that more formal methods for detection of important changes in military budget data could be used to complement the diplomatic histories for a somewhat more rigorous selection of the set of arms races studied. Applicable techniques include Box-Jenkins tests for stationarity, Harrison and Stevens' conversion of Kalman filtering, and Sard and Weintraub's cubic spline approximation methods.

APPENDIX II
The Domestic Pressure Question

A large portion of deterrence writing focuses on the domestic rather than the international factors affecting weapons competition. Hence the question arises whether an inquiry of this sort should not include greater consideration of the domestic factors which spur arming, especially in view of the influence of the military in foreign policy making worldwide. A full answer to this question would be developed from the following lines of argument:

1) **The apparently necessary choice between domestic and international arguments is based on a false dichotomy; domestic pressure arguments are logically prior to the international impacts arguments.**

Domestic factors are generally acknowledged to have an effect on most foreign policy. Thus it is not generally alleged that domestic concerns do not impact at all on arms racing, especially given the substantial domestic political and economic payoff potential of major weapons programs. (For example, the U.S. "Senator from Boeing" Jackson.) However, it is not necessary to refute the domestic pressure factor argument in order to advance research about effects of arming patterns assumed to be internationally reactive, given that they are not mutually exclusive arguments and given that the domestic pressure considerations are logically prior to the international effects of programs resulting from these pressures. (It is worth noting in this context that Richardson [1960a] intended to capture domestic effects in his arms race models.) Domestic pressure arguments and arms racing arguments are not mutually exclusive, but examine different aspects of the same issue. This contention has been researched by Choucri and North (1975), Holsti (1972) and others in various ways. In the case of war prediction or deterrence success/failure, the international weaponry comparisons are argued theoretically to be the proximal cause of war or peace outcomes, via crises, while domestic financial and other interests precede the international ones logically and temporally.

2) Exclusively domestic explanations of arming behavior are incomplete. (See Hempel's partial explanations, 1965:235, 416.)

Explanations of arming behavior based solely on domestic variables do not meet the criteria of complete explanations of arms racing; that is, they explain why some arming takes place, and may explain (completely) the distribution of contracts, etc., but they do not explain why specific adversaries are chosen (or dismissed) or why the consequent deployment and targeting patterns develop—in short, the international ramifications of the domestic process. This provides at best an incomplete international picture.

A part of the literature which, on excessively narrow logical grounds, advocates domestic factors as exclusive predictors of arming also suffers from some severe methodological shortcomings, despite the elegance of some of the underlying arguments. The most frequent sort of difficulty arises in the use of OLS statistics with lagged endogenous variables, though there appear to be some difficulties with operationalizations as well. The arms race connection argument cannot be refuted in these terms, nor does it actually need to be refuted for the authors to discuss the parameters of real domestic interactions on a country's defense preparations. Especially since military forces have differing domestic functions cross-nationally (Hammond, in Schilling, Hammond and Snyder, 1962; Huntington, 1958), such as guarding borders, creating employment for otherwise unemployed people, teaching reading and writing, and functioning as domestic police or disaster relief workers, the varied contributions of domestic interests to national arming programs deserve scrutiny.

3) Two of the "domestic determination of arming patterns" hypotheses seem to fail to square with the facts.

Results expected if decision makers manipulate military spending to enhance (i.e., either to prolong or increase the rewards of) their tenure in office do not seem to be forthcoming. (Note however, that this literature is largely limited to the U.S.) Russett (1964) found generally low relationships between measures of economic performance and military outlays. Thus, increasing Department of Defense (DOD) budgets had not, in the period studied by Russett, provided the economic payoffs which help keep a U.S. administration in office. Although there are some technical problems with their work, it is also worth noting that Cusack and Ward (1981:435) suggest there is only a weak ability in the U.S. for the chief executive to "regulate aggregate demand" via the DOD budget—since it is relatively inflexible—so as to provide an economic upsurge prior to major elections. (See also Frey, 1978; Tufte, 1978.)

Another summary view of this question can be obtained, somewhat crudely, via Figure 1. Suppose that the DOD budget is used for one fairly

96

straightforward purpose—for demand management, in which case DOD spending should be used against the U.S. business cycle to even out the effects of inflation and to stimulate growth. If this is so, when the business cycle is in a downturn, we should expect growth in DOD, and conversely. When graphed over time, the DOD budget should not co-vary importantly with measures of the business cycle, such as percentage change in U.S. GNP but should, if it is perfectly opposed to the business cycle, present a mirror image to percent change in GNP symmetric along some horizontal axis.

Several observations can be made on the basis of the graph in Figure 1. The first is that no matter what the domestic dynamics in arming, major surges in percentage change terms are strongly related to *international* events. Thus we have relative maxima in 1948 and 1949, after the World War II demobilization, and in time for the end of the Chinese civil war and the Soviet's first nuclear test (1949); in 1951, for the Korean War; and in 1966-1967, corresponding to the major upswings in the bombing in North Vietnam. There is also a major decrease in 1954 as the U.S. begins to rely on the massive retaliation doctrine.

Until 1954 there is a tendency for change in defense spending to *follow* changes in GNP, and apparently to respond to them, rather than the other way around. Throughout the rest of the period under study, GNP and defense outlays in percent change terms track one another fairly closely, increasing and decreasing at about the same time, or roughly synchronously, so that military spending does not appear to be used consistently counter-cyclically in these terms. If we define them as points where GNP diminishes and defense outlays are up, points of potential countercyclical use are given at 1956-1957 and 1959-1960. Neither do there seem to be persistent positive changes in presidential election years. These may not be the most appropriate terms in which to examine the countercyclical spending question, but they do suggest that at this level percent change in GNP appears to co-vary *with* percent change in military purchases rather than against it. (For a more detailed discussion see Nelson, 1976.)

Domestic pressure and internationally interactive arms racing views ought to be seen as complementary conceptualizations emphasizing differing aspects of the weapons acquisition process. In *Trojan Peace* I have down-played domestic pressure questions because the deterrence propositions tested do not rely on specification of domestic economic and political factors as aspects of national security or of a stable deterrent. Perhaps they should, so that a reasonable balance between a healthy economy and any necessary defense efforts could be better highlighted.

97

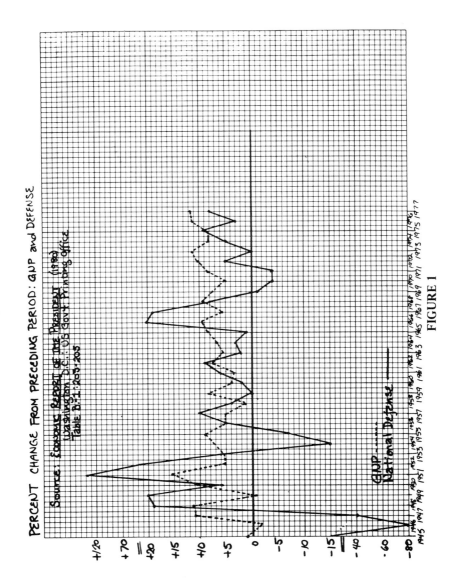

FIGURE 1

COLORADO COLLEGE LIBRARY
COLORADO SPRINGS,
COLORADO

2 CHILE - PERU   Current Prices, Local Currencies Estimates

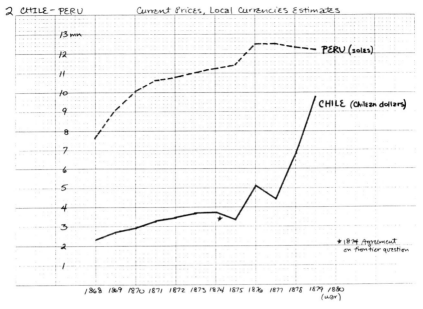

13 mn
12
11
10
9
8
7
6
5
4
3
2
1

PERU (soles)

CHILE (Chilean dollars)

★ 1874 Agreement
on frontier question

1868 1869 1870 1871 1872 1873 1874 1875 1876 1877 1878 1879 1880
(war)

3 GUATEMALA - EL SALVADOR   Current Price Figures, Local Currencies
(El Salvador serving as foil to Guatemala)

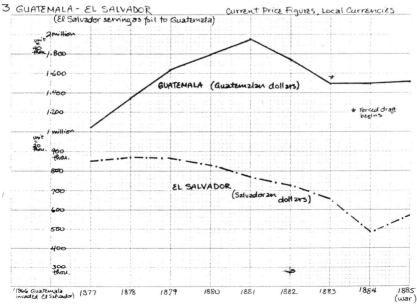

unit = 10 thou. 2 million
1,800
1,600
1,400
1,200
unit = 10 thou. 1 million
900 thou.
800
700
600
500
400
300 thou.

GUATEMALA (Guatemalan dollars)

EL SALVADOR
(Salvadoran dollars)

★ Forced draft begins

(1866 Guatemala invaded El Salvador) 1877 1878 1879 1880 1881 1882 1883 1884 1885
(war)

101

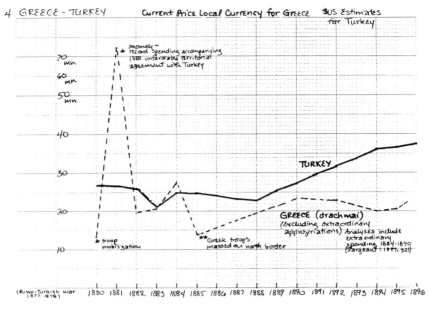

4 GREECE - TURKEY   Current Price Local Currency for Greece $US Estimates for Turkey

70 mn

★ anomaly –
record Spending accompanying
1881 unfavorable territorial
agreement with Turkey

60 mn

50 mn

40

30   TURKEY

20   GREECE (drachmai)
                                                        (excluding extraordinary
                                                        appropriations) Analyses include
                                                        extraordinary
★ troop   ★★ Greek troops   spending 1884-1890
mobilization   massed on north border   (Sargeant : 1897; 321)

10

(Russo-Turkish war   1880 1881 1882 1883 1884 1885 1886 1887 1888 1889 1890 1891 1892 1893 1894 1895 1896
1877-1878)

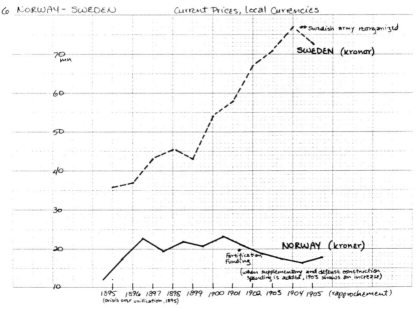

6 NORWAY - SWEDEN   Current Prices, local Currencies

                                                    ★★ Swedish army reorganized

70 mn   SWEDEN (kronor)

60

50

40

30

20   NORWAY (kroner)
                                    Fortification
                                    Funding
                                    (when supplementary and defense construction
                                    spending is added, 1903 shows an increase)
10

    1895 1896 1897 1898 1899 1900 1901 1902 1903 1904 1905 (rapprochement)
(crisis over unification, 1895)

102

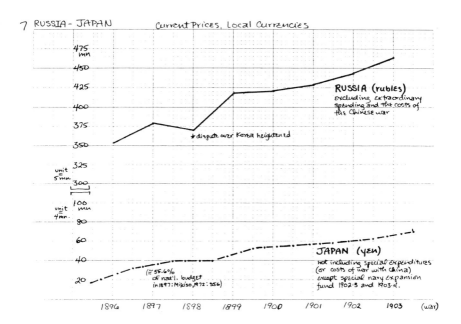

7 RUSSIA - JAPAN   Current Prices, Local Currencies

RUSSIA (rubles) excluding extraordinary spending and the costs of the Chinese war

* dispute over Korea heightened

unit = 5mn

unit = 4mn

JAPAN (yen) not including special expenditures (or costs of war with China) except special navy expansion fund 1902·3 and 1903·4.

(≈ 55.6% of nat'l. budget in 1897: Mikiso, 1972: 356)

1896 1897 1898 1899 1900 1901 1902 1903 (war)

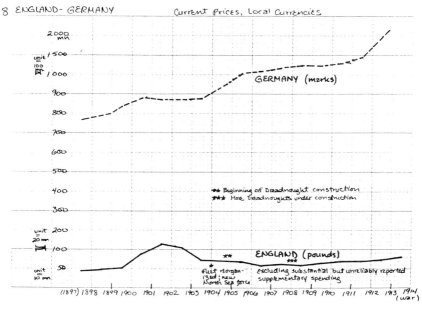

8 ENGLAND - GERMANY   Current Prices, Local Currencies

unit = 100 mn

GERMANY (marks)

** Beginning of Dreadnought construction
*** More Dreadnoughts under construction

unit = 20 mn

ENGLAND (pounds)

unit = 10 mn

* Fleet reorganized; new North Sea force
excluding substantial but unreliably reported supplementary spending

(1897) 1898 1899 1900 1901 1902 1903 1904 1905 1906 1907 1908 1909 1910 1911 1912 1913 1914 (war)

103

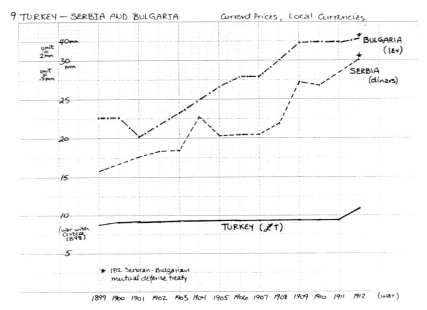

9 TURKEY — SERBIA AND BULGARIA   Current Prices, Local Currencies

unit
2mn

unit
= .5mn

40mn

30 mn

25

20

15

10

5

(war with
Greece
1898)

★ BULGARIA (lev)

★ SERBIA (dinars)

TURKEY (£T)

★ 1912 Serbian-Bulgarian mutual defense treaty

1899 1900 1901 1902 1903 1904 1905 1906 1907 1908 1909 1910 1911 1912 (war)

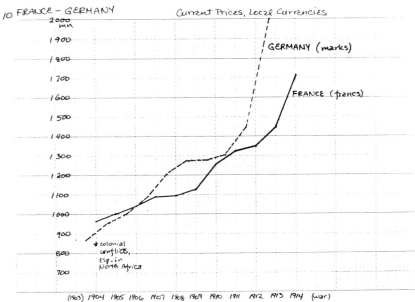

10 FRANCE — GERMANY   Current Prices, Local Currencies

2000 mn
1900
1800
1700
1600
1500
1400
1300
1200
1100
1000
900
800
700

GERMANY (marks)

FRANCE (francs)

★ colonial conflicts, esp. in North Africa

(1903) 1904 1905 1906 1907 1908 1909 1910 1911 1912 1913 1914 (war)

104

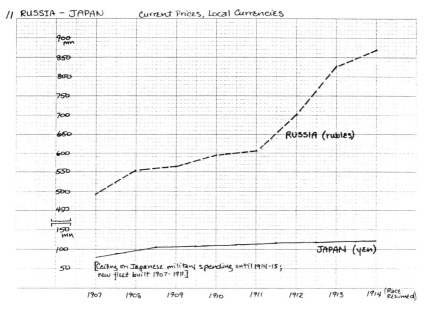

11 RUSSIA - JAPAN   Current Prices, Local Currencies

900 mn
850
800
750
700
650   RUSSIA (rubles)
600
550
500
450
150 mn
100   JAPAN (yen)
50   [Ceiling on Japanese military spending until 1914-15;
          new fleet built 1907-1911.]

          1907   1908   1909   1910   1911   1912   1913   1914 [Race Resumed]

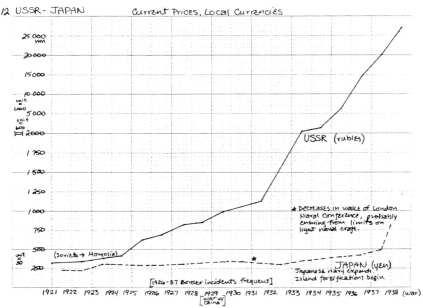

12 USSR - JAPAN   Current Prices, Local Currencies

25 000 mn
20 000
15 000
10 000
unit = 1,000 5000
unit = 600 2000   USSR (rubles)
1 750
1 500
1 250
1 000   * Decreases in wake of London
                                     Naval Conference, probably
750   ensuing from limits on
                                     light naval craft.
500
unit = 50 250   (Soviets → Mongolia)
                                              JAPAN (yen)
          [1926-37 Border incidents frequent]   Japanese navy expands,
                                                 Island fortifications begin

1921 1922 1923 1924 1925 1926 1927 1928 1929 1930 1931 1932 1933 1934 1935 1936 1937 1938 (war)
                                      [war w/ China]

105

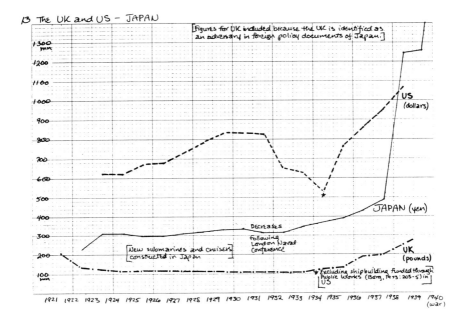

13 The UK and US - JAPAN

[Figures for UK included because the UK is identified as an adversary in foreign policy documents of Japan.]

1300 mn
1200
1100
1000
900
800
700
600
500
400
300
200
100 mn

US (dollars)

JAPAN (yen)

DECREASES

Following London Naval Conference

New submarines and cruisers constructed in Japan

UK (pounds)

*Excluding shipbuilding funded through Public Works (Berg, 1973: 205-5) in US

1921 1922 1923 1924 1925 1926 1927 1928 1929 1930 1931 1932 1933 1934 1935 1936 1937 1938 1939 1940 (war)

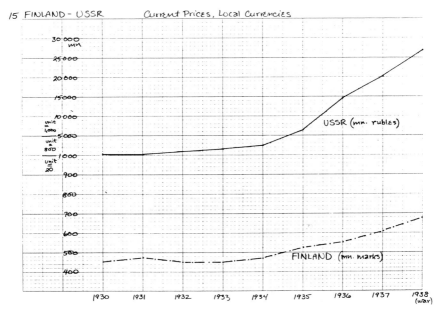

15 FINLAND - USSR   Current Prices, Local Currencies

30 000 mn
25 000
20 000
15 000
10 000
unit = 1,000 5 000
unit = 800 1 000
unit = 20 900
800
700
600
500
400

USSR (mn. rubles)

FINLAND (mn. marks)

1930   1931   1932   1933   1934   1935   1936   1937   1938 (war)

106

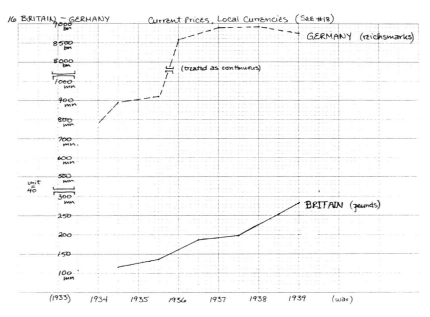

16 BRITAIN — GERMANY   Current Prices, Local Currencies   (SEE #18)

GERMANY (reichsmarks)

(treated as continuous)

BRITAIN (pounds)

unit
= 40

7000 bn
8500 bn
8000 bn
7000 mn
900 mn
800 mn
700 mn.
600 mn
500 mn
300 mn
250
200
150
100 mn

(1933)   1934   1935   1936   1937   1938   1939   (war)

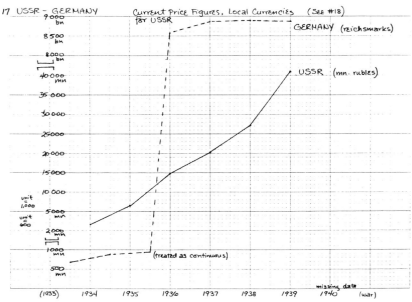

17 USSR — GERMANY   Current Price Figures, Local Currencies   (SEE #18)

for USSR

GERMANY (reichsmarks)

USSR (mn. rubles)

(treated as continuous)

unit
1,000

unit
= 600

9000 bn
8500 bn
8000 bn
40000 mn
35000
30000
25000
20000
15000
10000
5000 mn
2000 mn
1000 mn
500 mn

missing data

(1933)   1934   1935   1936   1937   1938   1939   1940   (war)

107

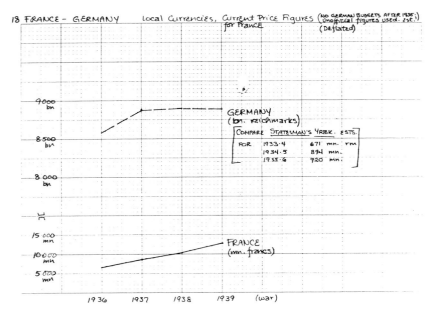

18 FRANCE - GERMANY   Local Currencies, Current Price Figures (NO GERMAN BUDGETS AFTER 1935;)
                                              for France   (Unofficial figures used. est.)
                                                                            (Deflated)

9000
bn

8500
bn   GERMANY
                            (bn. Reichmarks)
                            COMPARE STATESMAN'S YRBK. ESTS.
8000   FOR   1933·4   671 mn. rm
bn   1934·5   894 mn.
                                  1935·6   920 mn.

15 000
mn   FRANCE
10 000   (mn. francs)
mn
5 000
mn

        1936   1937   1938   1939   (war)

19 USA - USSR   Current Price Figures, Local Currencies

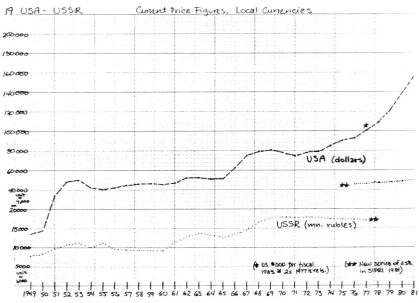

200000
180000
160000
140000
120 000
100000
80 000   USA (dollars)
60000
40000
unit   **
= 4,000
20000
15000   USSR (mn. rubles)   **
10000

5000
unit
= 1000   (* US $000 for fiscal   (** New series of ests.
                         1983 ≈ 2x 1977 levels.)   in SIPRI 1981)

1949 '50 '51 52 53 54 55 56 57 58 59 60 61 62 63 64 65 66 67 68 69 70 71 72 73 74 75 76 77 78 79 80 81

108

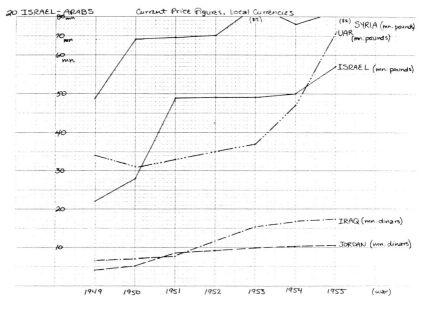

20 ISRAEL-ARABS   Current Price Figures, Local Currencies

(82) SYRIA (mn. pounds)
UAR (mn. pounds)
ISRAEL (mn. pounds)
IRAQ (mn. dinars)
JORDAN (mn. dinars)

1949   1950   1951   1952   1953   1954   1955   (war)

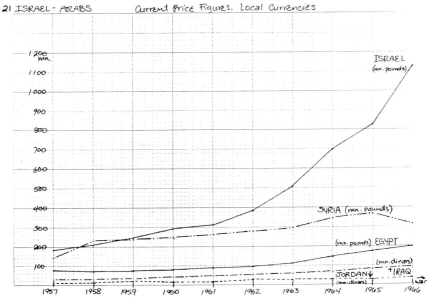

21 ISRAEL-ARABS   Current Price Figures, Local Currencies

ISRAEL (mn. pounds)
SYRIA (mn. pounds)
(mn. pounds) EGYPT
(mn. dinars) IRAQ
JORDAN (mn. dinars)

1957   1958   1959   1960   1961   1962   1963   1964   1965   1966

109

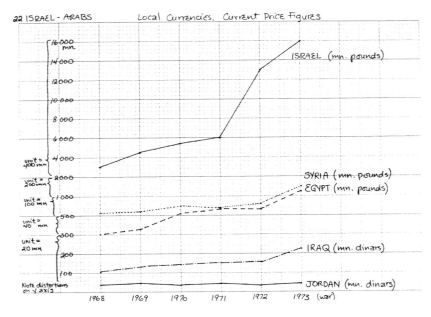

22 ISRAEL - ARABS   Local Currencies, Current Price Figures

16.000 mn.
14.000   ISRAEL (mn. pounds)
12.000
10.000
8.000
6.000
unit = 400mn   4.000
unit = 200mn   2.000   SYRIA (mn. pounds)
unit = 100 mn   1.000   EGYPT (mn. pounds)
unit = 40 mn   500
unit = 20 mn   300
                200   IRAQ (mn. dinars)
                100
Note distortions
on Y axis   JORDAN (mn. dinars)
        1968   1969   1970   1971   1972   1973 (war)

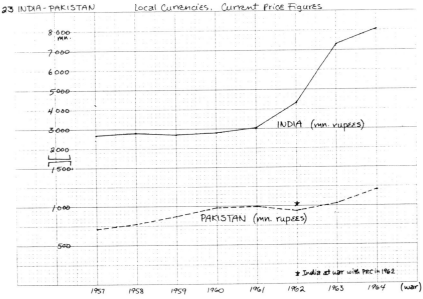

23 INDIA - PAKISTAN   Local Currencies, Current Price Figures

8.000 mn.
7.000
6.000
5.000
4.000
3.000   INDIA (mn. rupees)
2.000
1.500
1.000
        PAKISTAN (mn. rupees)
500
        ★ India at war with PRC in 1962
        1957   1958   1959   1960   1961   1962   1963   1964   (war)

110

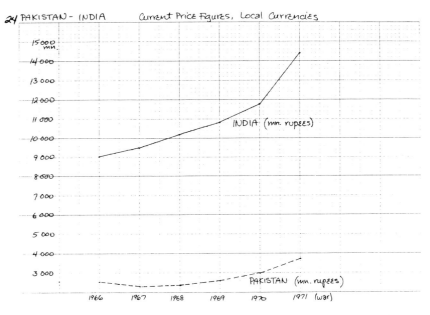

24 PAKISTAN - INDIA   Current Price Figures, Local Currencies

15 000 mn
14 000
13 000
12 000
11 000
10 000
9 000
8 000
7 000
6 000
5 000
4 000
3 000

INDIA (mn. rupees)

PAKISTAN (mn. rupees)

1966   1967   1968   1969   1970   1971 (war)

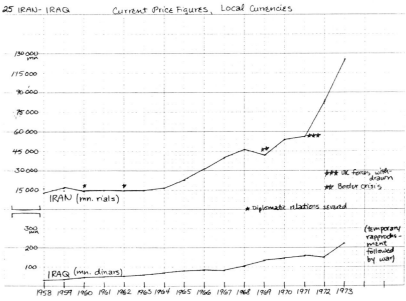

25 IRAN - IRAQ   Current Price Figures, Local Currencies

130 000 mn
115 000
90 000
75 000
60 000
45 000
30 000
15 000

IRAN (mn. rials)

***
**
*

*** UK forces with-
      drawn
** Border crisis
* Diplomatic relations severed

300 mn
200
100

IRAQ (mn. dinars)

(temporary
rapproche-
ment
followed
by war)

1958 1959 1960 1961 1962 1963 1964 1965 1966 1967 1968 1969 1970 1971 1972 1973

111

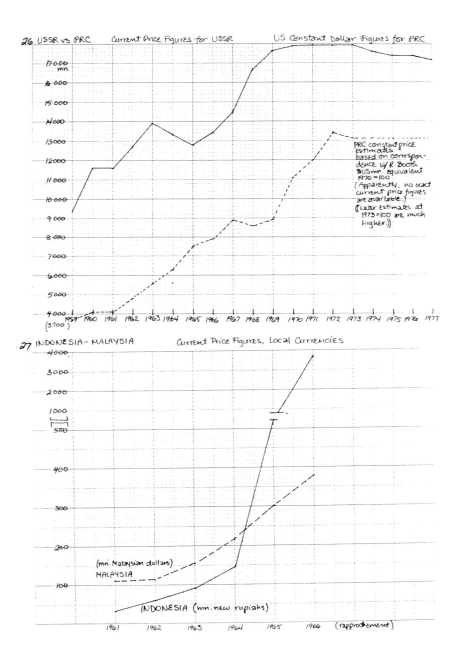

26 USSR vs PRC   Current Price Figures for USSR   US Constant Dollar Figures for PRC

17000 mn
16000
15000
14000
13000
12000
11000
10000
9000
8000
7000
6000
5000
4000
(3700)

1959 1960 1961 1962 1963 1964 1965 1966 1967 1968 1969 1970 1971 1972 1973 1974 1975 1976 1977

PRC constant price
estimates
based on correspon-
dence w/ R. Booth
$US mn. equivalent
1970 = 100
(Apparently, no exact
current price figures
are available.)
((Later estimates at
1973 = 100 are much
higher.))

27 INDONESIA - MALAYSIA   Current Price Figures, Local Currencies

4000
3000
2000
1000
500

400
300
200
100

(mn. Malaysian dollars)
MALAYSIA

INDONESIA (mn. new rupiahs)

1961   1962   1963   1964   1965   1966   (rapprochement)

112

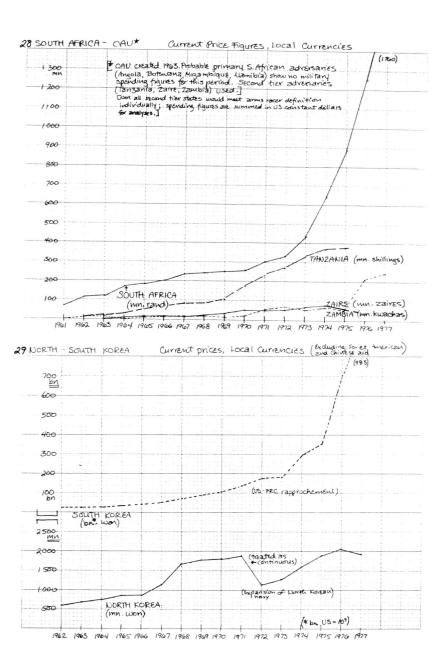

28 SOUTH AFRICA - OAU*   Current Price Figures, Local Currencies

(1760)

+ 300 mn
+ 200
1100
1000
900
800
700
600
500
400
300
200
100

* OAU created 1963. Probable primary S. African adversaries (Angola, Botswana, Mozambique, Namibia) show no military spending figures for this period. Second tier adversaries (Tanzania, Zaire, Zambia) used.]
[Not all second tier states would meet arms racer definition individually; spending figures are summed in US constant dollars for analyses.]

TANZANIA (mn. shillings)

SOUTH AFRICA (mn. rand)

ZAIRE (mn. zaires)
ZAMBIA (mn. kwachas)

1961 1962 1963 1964 1965 1966 1967 1968 1969 1970 1971 1972 1973 1974 1975 1976 1977

29 NORTH - SOUTH KOREA   Current prices, Local Currencies (Excluding Soviet American, and Chinese aid)

(985)

700 bn
600
500
400
300
200
100 bn

(US-PRC rapprochement)

SOUTH KOREA (bn.* won)

2500 mn
2000
1500
1000
500

(treated as continuous)

(expansion of North Korean navy)

NORTH KOREA (mn. won)

(* bn US = 10⁹)

1962 1963 1964 1965 1966 1967 1968 1969 1970 1971 1972 1973 1974 1975 1976 1977

113

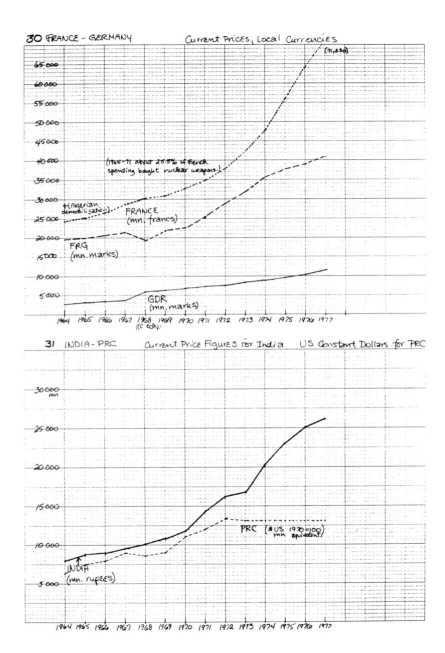

30 FRANCE - GERMANY   Current Prices, Local Currencies

65 000

60 000

55 000

50 000

45 000

40 000

35 000

30 000

25 000

20 000

15 000

10 000

5 000

(71,830)

(1965-71 about 25.5% of French
spending bought nuclear weapons.)

+(Algerian
demobilisation)

FRANCE
(mn. francs)

FRG
(mn. marks)

GDR
(mn. marks)

1964 1965 1966 1967 1968 1969 1970 1971 1972 1973 1974 1975 1976 1977
                    ((c.econ))

31 INDIA - PRC   Current Price Figures for India   US Constant Dollars for PRC

30 000
mn

25 000

20 000

15 000

10 000

5 000

PRC ($ US 1970=100)
     mn. equivalent)

INDIA
(mn. rupees)

1964 1965 1966 1967 1968 1969 1970 1971 1972 1973 1974 1975 1976 1977

114

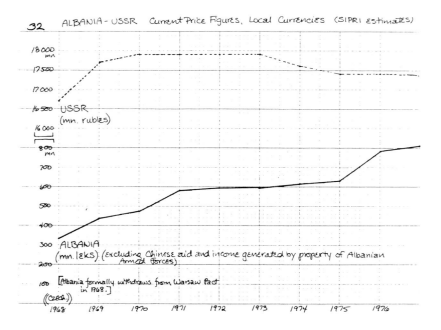

32   ALBANIA - USSR   Current Price Figures, Local Currencies (SIPRI estimates)

18 000 mn
17 500
17 000
16 500 USSR
        (mn. rubles)
16 000
800 mn
700
600
500
400
300 ALBANIA
     (mn. leks) (excluding Chinese aid and income generated by property of Albanian
200   Armed Forces)

100 [Albania formally withdraws from Warsaw Pact
         in 1968.]
((Czech.))

1968   1969   1970   1971   1972   1973   1974   1975   1976

REFERENCES*

Abolfathi, F. 1975. Obstacles to the Quantitative Analysis of Public Expenditures Policies: The Case of Military Spending. Arlington: Consolidated Analysis Centers, Inc. (mimeo).

Albertini, L. 1928. *The Origins of the War of 1914*. London: Oxford University Press.

Alcock, N. 1972. *The War Disease*. Oaksville, Ontario: Canadian Peace Research Institute Press.

Alcock, N., and Young, C. 1973. Evidence of an Epochal Cycle. *Peace Research* 4:68-74.

Alexandroff, A., and Rosecrance, R. 1977. Deterrence in 1939. *World Politics* 29:3.

Aron, R. 1959. Trans. T. Kilmartin. *On War*. Garden City: Doubleday.

Baldwin, D. A. 1971. The Power of Positive Sanctions. *World Politics* 24:19-38.

Banks, A. S. 1971. *Cross-Polity Time Series Data*. Cambridge: Massachusetts Institute of Technology Press.

Barros, M.V.B. 1970. *Historia Diplomatica de Chile 1541-1939*. Barcelona: Ediciones Ariel.

Baylis, H., and Segal, G., eds. 1981. *Soviet Strategy*. London: Croom Helm, and Montclair, NJ: Allanheld, Osmun Inc.

Beer, F. A. ed. 1970. *Alliances: Latent War Communities in the Contemporary World*. New York: Holt, Rinehart & Winston.

Beilenson, L. W., and Cohen, S. T. 1982. A New Nuclear Strategy. *New York Times Magazine* 24 January:36.

Berezhkov, V. 1962. The "Auto-Accident" Theory of War. *New Times*. Moscow, 18 April:18.

Berkson, J. 1955. Maximum Likelihood and Minimum Chi-Square Estimates of the Logistic Function. *Journal of American Statistical Association* 50:529-49.

─────────────

*A separate bibliography used to make status quo-revisionist determinations is available from the author.

Bobrow, D., ed. 1969. *Weapons System Decisions*. New York: Praeger.

Bondarenko, V. M. 1966. Military-Technical Superiority: The Most Important Factor in the Reliable Defense of the Country. In *Kommunist Vooruzhennikh Sil* (Communist of the Armed Forces), September. Trans. and reprinted in Kintner and Scott (1967), *The Nuclear Revolution in Soviet Military Affairs*. Norman: University of Oklahoma Press.

Booth, K. 1979. *Strategy and Ethnocentrism*. New York: Holmes & Meier.

Borg, D.; Okamoto, S.; Finlayson, D.K.A. 1973. *Pearl Harbor as History: Japanese American Relations 1931-1941*. New York: Columbia University Press.

Brezhnev, L. 1973. *Krasnaya Zvezda* 28 March.

Brodie, B. 1973. *War and Politics*. New York: Macmillan.

Brodie, B., and Brodie, F. 1973. 2nd ed. *From Crossbow to H. Bomb*. Bloomington: Indiana University Press.

Bryan, J. G. 1950. *A Method for the Exact Determination of the Characteristic Equation and Latent Vectors of a Matrix*. Cambridge: Harvard University.

Burt, R. 1981. NATO and Nuclear Deterrence. Speech before Arms Control Association Conference, Brussels, 23 Sept. Reprinted *U.S. Department of State Current Policy, No. 319*. Washington, DC: U.S. Department of State Bureau of Public Affairs.

Cantor, G. 1955. Trans. Philip E. B. Jourdain. The Arithmetic of Infinite and Transfinite Numbers. In *Contributions to the Sounding of the Theory of Transfinite Numbers*. New York: Dover.

Carr, E. H. 1937. *International Relations Since the Peace Treaties*. London: Macmillan.

_____. 1946. *The Twenty Years' Crisis*. New York: Harper and Row.

_____. 1947. *Conditions of Peace*. New York: Macmillan.

Caspary, W. R. 1967. Richardson's Model of Arms Races: Description, Critique, and an Alternative Model. *International Studies Quarterly* II:1.

Cerf, J. H., and Pozen, W., eds. 1961. *Strategy for the Sixties*. New York: Praeger.

Choucri, N., and North, R. C. 1975. *Nations in Conflict*. San Francisco: W. H. Freeman.

Cleary, P. 1980. Analyzing Relationships Involving a Dichotomous Dependent Variable. New Brunswick: Rutgers, The State University of New Jersey. (Mimeo).

Coffey, J. I. 1971. *Deterrence in the 1970s*. Denver: University of Denver Monograph Series in World Affairs.

Cox, A. M. 1976. *The Dynamics of Detente*. New York: W. W. Norton.

Cox, D. 1970. *The Analysis of Binary Data*. London: Methuen.

Crowley, J. B. 1966. *Japan's Quest for Autonomy.* Princeton: Princeton University Press.

Cusack, T. R., and Ward, M. D. 1981. Military Spending in the U.S., the Soviet Union and the PRC. *Journal of Conflict Resolution* 25:429-69.

Dallin, D. 1961. *Soviet Foreign Policy after Stalin.* Philadelphia: J. B. Lippincott.

Deutsch, K. 1968. A Critique of Deterrence Theory. In *The Analysis of International Relations.* New York: Prentice-Hall. Reprinted in Art, R. J., and Jervis, R. (1973), *International Politics: Anarchy, Force, Imperialism.* Boston: Little, Brown.

Doran, C. F. 1973. A Theory of Bounded Deterrence. *Journal of Conflict Resolution* 17:243-69.

Dougherty, J. E., and J. F. Lehman, Jr., eds. 1965. *Prospects for Arms Control.* New York: Macfadden-Bartell.

Douglass, J. D., Jr. 1980. *Soviet Military Strategy in Europe.* New York: Pergamon.

Douglass, J. D., Jr., and Hoeber, A. M. 1970. *Soviet Strategy for Nuclear War.* Stanford: Hoover Institution Press.

Dreher, C. 1958. War by Accident. *The Nation* 107:6.

Dror, Y. 1971. *Crazy States.* Lexington: D. C. Heath.

Eisenstein, J., and Jacob, H. 1977. *Felony Justice.* Boston: Little, Brown.

Ellsberg, D. 1960. *The Crude Analysis of Strategic Choices.* Santa Monica: Rand Unclassified P-2183 and in *American Economic Review*, May 1961, LI:472-78.

_____. 1961. *Risk, Ambiguity and the Savage Axioms.* Santa Monica: Rand Unclassified P-2173 and in *Quarterly Journal of Economics*, November 1961:643-69.

_____. 1968. *The Theory and Practice of Blackmail.* Santa Monica: Rand Unclassified P-3883.

Etzioni, A. 1964. *Winning without War.* Garden City: Doubleday.

Fink, C. F. 1965. More Calculations about Deterrence. *Journal of Conflict Resolution* 9:54-95.

Fisher, R. A. 1936. The Use of Multiple Measurements in Taxonomic Problems. *Annals of Eugenics* 8:179-88.

Frank, L. A. 1977. *Soviet Nuclear Planning: A Point of View on SALT.* Washington, DC: American Enterprise Institute for Public Policy Research.

Freedman, L. 1977. *U.S. Intelligence and the Soviet Strategic Threat.* London: Macmillan.

Frey, B. 1978. *Modern Political Economy.* London: Martin and Robinson.

Gallois, P. 1961. Trans. Richard Howard. *The Balance of Terror: Strategy for the Nuclear Age*. Boston: Houghton Mifflin.

Garthoff, R. L. 1962. *Soviet Strategy in the Nuclear Age*. New York: Praeger.

George, A., and Smoke, R. 1974. *Deterrence in American Foreign Policy: Theory and Practice*. New York: Columbia University Press.

Gilbert, E. S. 1968. On Discrimination Using Qualitative Variables. *Journal of the American Statistical Association* 63:1399-1412.

Gilbert, S. P., ed. 1977. *Soviet Images of America*. New York: Crane Russak.

Goldberger, A. 1964. *Econometric Theory*. New York: John Wiley & Sons.

Goldhamer, H. 1971. *The Soviet Union in a Period of Strategic Parity*. Santa Monica: Rand R-889-PR.

_____. 1979. *Reality and Belief in Military Affairs*. Santa Monica: Rand R-2448-NA.

Goure, L.; Kohler, F.; and Harvey, M. 1974. *The Role of Nuclear Forces in Current Soviet Strategy*. Miami: University of Miami Press.

Gray, C. 1971. The Arms Race Phenomenon. *World Politics* 24:39-79.

_____. 1976. *The Soviet-American Arms Race*. Westmead, England: Saxon House, D. C. Heath and Lexington: D. C. Heath.

Green, P. 1966. *Deadly Logic: The Theory of Nuclear Deterrence*. Columbus: Ohio State University Press.

Hahn, W. F., and Neff, J. C., eds. 1960. *American Strategy for the Nuclear Age*. Garden City: Doubleday.

Halperin, M. H. 1963. *Limited War in the Nuclear Age*. New York: John Wiley & Sons.

_____. 1971. *Defense Strategies for the 70's*. Boston: Little, Brown.

Halperin, M. H., and Kanter, A. 1973. *Readings in American Foreign Policy*. Boston: Little, Brown.

Halperin, M. H.; Plackwelder, W. C.; and Verter, J. I. 1971. Estimation of the Multivariate Logistic Risk Function: A Comparison of the Discriminant Function and Maximum Likelihood Approaches. *Journal of Chronic Diseases* 24:125-58.

Hanushek, E. A., and Jackson, J. E. 1977. *Statistical Methods for Social Scientists*. New York: Academic Press.

Hart, B. H. Liddell. 1960. *Deterrent or Defense?* New York: Praeger.

Hempel, C. 1965. *Aspects of Scientific Explanation*. New York: Free Press.

Hermann, D. C., ed. 1972. *International Crises: Insights from Behavioral Research*. New York: Free Press.

Holsti, O. R. 1972. *Crisis Escalation War*. Montreal: McGill-Queen's University Press.

Hopmann, P. T. 1972. Internal and External Influences on Bargaining in Arms Control Negotiations. In *Peace, War and Numbers*, ed. B. Russett, pp. 213-237. Beverly Hills: Sage.

Horelick, A. L., and Rush, M. 1965. *Strategic Power and Soviet Foreign Policy*. Chicago: University of Chicago Press.

Huntington, S. P. 1958. Arms Races: Prerequisites and Results. *Public Policy* 8:41-86.

_____. 1961. *The Common Defense*. New York: Columbia University Press.

Hurewitz, J. C. 1969. *Middle East Politics: The Military Dimension*. New York: Praeger.

Jabber, F. 1971. *Israel and Nuclear Weapons*. London: Chatto and Windus for the International Institute for Strategic Studies.

Jervis, R. 1976. *Perception and Misperception in International Politics*. Princeton: Princeton University Press.

_____. 1979. Deterrence Theory Revisited. *World Politics* 31:289-324.

_____. 1980. Why Nuclear Superiority Doesn't Matter. *Political Science Quarterly* 94:617-33.

Jones, W. M. 1974a. *A Framework for Exploring Escalation Control*. Santa Monica: Rand R-1536-RC.

_____. 1974b. *Modelling Soviet Behavior and Deterrence: A Procedure for Evaluating Military Forces*. Santa Monica: Rand R-1065-PR.

Kahn, H. 1960. The Arms Race and Some of Its Hazards. *Daedalus* 89: 744-80.

_____. 1964. *Thinking about the Unthinkable*. New York: Avon.

Kavic, L. J. 1967. *India's Quest for Security: Defense Politics 1947-1965*. Berkeley: University of California Press.

Kaysen, C. 1968. Keeping the Strategic Balance. *Foreign Affairs* 46:665-75.

Kemp, G.; Pfaltzgraff, R. L., Jr.; and Ra'Anan, U., eds. 1974. *The Superpowers in a Multinuclear World*. Lexington: D. C. Heath.

Kintner, W. A. 1967. *Peace and the Strategy Conflict*. New York: Praeger.

Kintner, W. R., and Scott, H. F., eds. and trans. 1968. *The Nuclear Revolution in Soviet Military Affairs*. Norman: University of Oklahoma Press.

Kissinger, H. A. 1960. Arms Control, Inspection and Surprise Attack. *Foreign Affairs* 38:557-75.

Klecka, W. R. 1975. The Clientele of Australian Parties: New Perspectives Through Discriminant Analysis. *Politics* 7:39.

_____. 1980. *Discriminant Analysis*. Sage University Paper No. 19 Series No. 07-019. Beverly Hills and London: Sage.

Klineberg, O. 1965. *The Human Dimension in International Relations*. New York: Holt, Rinehart & Winston.

Knorr, K. 1966. *On the Uses of Military Power in the Nuclear Age*. Princeton: Princeton University Press.

Kolodziej, E. A. 1966. *The Uncommon Defense and Congress 1945-1963*. Columbus: Ohio State University Press.

Kulakov, B. M. 1970. *Idologiia Agressi*. Moscow: Defense Ministry Military Press.

Lambeth, B. 1972. Deterrence in the MIRV Era. *World Politics* 24:221.

Lefever, E. W. 1979. *Nuclear Arms in the Third World*. Washington, DC: Brookings.

Lider, J. 1977. *On the Nature of War*. Swedish Institute of International Affairs. Westmead, England: Saxon House.

Liska, G. 1971. *Quest for Equilibrium: America and the Balance of Power on Land and Sea*. Baltimore: Johns Hopkins University Press.

Lowe, G. E. 1964. *The Age of Deterrence*. Boston: Little, Brown.

Lyons, G. H., and Morton, L. 1965. *Schools for Strategy: Education and Research in National Security Affairs*. New York: Praeger.

Marantz, P. 1975. Prelude to Detente: Doctrinal Change under Khrushchev. *International Studies Quarterly* 19:4.

McFadden, D. 1976. A Comment of Discriminant Analysis "versus" Logit Analysis. *Annals of Economic and Social Measurement* 5:511-24.

McNamara, R. S. 1968. *The Essence of Security*. New York: Harper & Row.

Midlarsky, M. 1974. Power, Uncertainty and the Onset of International Violence. *Journal of Conflict Resolution* 18:395-431.

Mikiso, H. 1972. *Japan: A Historical Survey*. New York: Charles Scribner's.

Mirchandani, G. G. 1968. *India's Nuclear Dilemma*. New York: Humanities Press and New Delhi: Popular Book Service.

Moll, K. 1974. International Conflict as a Decision System. *Journal of Conflict Resolution* 18:557-77.

Morley, J. W., trans. and ed. 1976. *Deterrent Diplomacy, from Taiheiyo sense e no michi: kaisen gaiko shi*. New York: Columbia University Press.

Naroll, R. 1964. Warfare, Peaceful Intercourse and Territorial Change: A Cross-Cultural Survey. Evanston: Northwestern University. (Mimeo).

_____. 1969. Deterrence in History. In *Theory and Research on the Causes of War*, eds. D. G. Pruitt and R. C. Snyder. Englewood Cliffs: Prentice-Hall.

Naroll, R.; Benjamin, E. D.; Fohr, F. K.; Fried, M. J.; Hildreth, R. D.; and Schaefer, J. M. 1971. Creativity: A Cross-Historical Pilot Study. *Journal of Cross-Cultural Psychology* 2:181-88.

Naroll, F.; Bullough, V. L.; and Naroll, F. 1974. *Military Deterrence in History: A Pilot Cross-Historical Survey*. Albany: State University of New York Press.

122

Nelson, D. 1976. The Cold War System: US-Soviet Relations 1946-1976. Master's Thesis. Chapel Hill: University of North Carolina.

Nerlove, M., and Press, S. J. 1973. *Univariate and Multivariate Log Linear and Logistic Models.* Santa Monica: Rand.

Nitze, P. 1976-1977. Deterring Our Deterrent. *Foreign Policy* 25:232.

Oppenheimer, J. R. 1963. *The Open Mind.* 2nd ed. New York: Simon & Schuster.

Osgood, C. 1962. *An Alternative to War or Surrender.* Urbana: University of Illinois Press.

Owen, D. 1972. *The Politics of Defense.* New York: Taplinger.

Pfister, J. W. 1974. *The Compulsion to War.* Beverly Hills and London: Sage.

Power, T. S. 1964. *Design for Survival.* New York: Coward, McCann & Geoghegan.

Press, S. J., and Wilson, S. 1978. Choosing Between Logistic Regression and Discriminant Analysis. *Journal of the American Statistical Association* 73:699-705.

Quandt, W. B. 1976. *Soviet Policy in the October 1973 War.* Santa Monica: Rand R-1864-ISA.

Quester, G. H. 1966. *Deterrence before Hiroshima: The Airpower Background of Modern Strategy.* New York: John Wiley & Sons.

Rapoport, A. 1960. *Fights, Games and Debates.* Ann Arbor: University of Michigan Press.

_____. 1964. *Strategy and Conscience.* Ann Arbor: University of Michigan Press.

Reagan, R. 1981. *U.S. Strategic Weapons Programs.* Department of State Bulletin 81:2057.

Richardson, L. F. 1960a. *Arms and Insecurity: A Mathematical Study of the Causes and Origins of War.* Pittsburgh: Boxwood Press.

_____. 1960b. *Statistics of Deadly Quarrels.* Pittsburgh: Boxwood Press.

Rummel, R. J. 1976. *Peace Endangered: The Reality of Detente.* Beverly Hills: Sage.

Russett, B. M. 1963. The Calculus of Deterrence. *Journal of Conflict Resolution* 7:-97-109.

_____. 1964. Measures of Military Effort. *American Behavioral Scientist* 7:26-29.

_____. 1967. Pearl Harbor: Deterrence Theory and Decision Theory. *Journal of Peace Research* 2:89.

Sallagar, F. M. 1980. *An Overview of the Soviet Threat.* Santa Monica: Rand R-2580-AF.

Saris, W., and Middendorp, C. 1980. Arms Races: External Security of Domestic Pressure. *British Journal of Political Science* 10:121-28.

Schelling, T. C. 1960. *The Strategy of Conflict*. Oxford: Oxford University Press.

_____. 1966. *Arms and Influence*. New Haven: Yale University Press.

Schilling, W. R.; Hammond, P. Y., and Snyder, G. 1962. *Strategy, Politics and Defense Budgets*. New York: Columbia University Press.

Schlesinger, J. R. 1974. The New Arms Race. *Time*, 11 February:20.

Sergeant, L. 1897. *Greece in the 19th Century*. London: T. Fisher Unwin.

Singer, J. D. 1962. *Deterrence, Arms Control and Disarmament: Toward a Synthesis in National Security Policy*. Columbus: Ohio State University Press.

Singer, J. R., and Small, M. 1972. *The Wages of War 1816-1965: A Statistical Handbook*. New York: John Wiley & Sons.

Singer, J. D.; Bremer, S.; and Stuckey, J. 1972. Capability Distribution, Uncertainty, and Major Power War, 1820-1965. In *Peace, War, and Numbers*, ed. B. M. Russett, pp. 19-48. Beverly Hills: Sage.

Smoke, R. 1977. *War: Controlling Escalation*. Cambridge: Harvard University Press.

Snyder, G. H. 1961. *Deterrence and Defense: Toward a Theory of National Security*. Princeton: Princeton University Press.

Sokolovsky, V. V. 1975. Marshall of the Soviet Union. In *Soviet Military Strategy*, ed. H. F. Scott. New York: Crane, Russak.

Spadolini, G. 1981. *New York Times*, 13 September:20.

Speed, R. 1979. *Strategic Deterrence in the 1980s*. Stanford: Hoover Institution.

Steiner, B. 1973. *Arms Races, Diplomacy and Recurring Behavior*. Sage Professional Paper. Beverly Hills: Sage.

Stockholm International Peace Research Institute. 1977, 1978. *World Armaments and Disarmament SIPRI Yearbooks 1977, 1978*. Stockholm: Almquist and Wiksell International.

Subrahmanyam, K. 1974. An Indian Nuclear Force in the Eighties. In *The Superpowers in a Multinuclear World*, eds. G. Kemp; R. L. Pflatzgraff, Jr.; and U. R'anan. Lexington: D. C. Heath.

Tatsuoka, M. M. 1970. *Discriminant Analysis: The Study of Group Differences*. Champagne, IL: Institute for Personality and Ability Testing.

_____. 1971. *Multivariate Analysis: Techniques for Educational and Psychological Research*. New York: John Wiley & Sons.

Taylor, A.J.P. 1961. *The Origins of the Second World War*. New York: Fawcett.

Theil, H. 1969. A Multinomial Extension of the Linear Logit Model. *International Economic Review* 10:251-59.

_____. 1971. *Principles of Econometrics*. New York: John Wiley & Sons.

Triska, J. F., and Finley, D. D. 1968. *Soviet Foreign Policy*. New York: Macmillan.

Tufte, E. 1978. *The Political Control of the Economy*. Princeton: Princeton University Press.

Voevodsky, J. 1969. Quantitative Behavior of Warring Nations. *Journal of Psychology* 72:269-92.

_____. 1970. Quantitative Analysis of Nations at War. *Peace Research Review* 3:1-21.

_____. 1972. Crisis Waves: Growth and Decline of War-Related Behavioral Events. *Journal of Psychology* 80:289-308.

Wallace, M. D. 1971. Power, Status and International War. *Journal of Peace Research* 1:23-35.

_____. 1972. Status, Formal Organization and Arms Levels as Factors Leading to the Onset of War, 1820-1924. In *Peace, War, and Numbers*, ed. B. M. Russett, Beverly Hills and London: Sage.

_____. 1976. Arms Races and the Balance of Power: A Preliminary Mathematical Model. *Applied Mathematical Modelling* 1:2.

_____. 1979. Arms Races and Escalation: Some New Evidence. *Journal of Conflict Resolution* 23:3-16.

_____. 1980. Some Persisting Findings: A Reply to Professor Weede. *Journal of Conflict Resolution* 24:289-92.

_____. 1981. Old Nails in New Coffins: The Para Bellum Hypothesis Revisited. *Journal of Peace Research* 18:91-95.

Wallace, M. D., and Wilson, J. M. 1978. Nonlinear Arms Race Models. *Journal of Peace Research* 15:175-92.

Walters, R. E. 1974. *The Nuclear Trap: An Escape Route*. Middlesex, England: Penguin Books.

Weede, E. 1980. Arms Races and Escalation: Some Persisting Doubts. *Journal of Conflict Resolution* 24:285-88.

Weinberger, C. W. 1981. *Requirements of Our Defense Policy*. U.S. Department of State Bulletin 81:2052.

Weiss, J. D. 1972. Multivariate Procedures. In *Handbook of Industrial and Organizational Psychology*, ed. M.D.V. Dunnette, Chicago: Rand McNally.

White, R. K. 1965. The Genuineness of Soviet Elite Fear of U.S. Aggression. In *Weapons System Decisions*, ed. D. B. Bobrow, New York: Washington and London: Praeger.

Whiting, A. S. 1975. *The Chinese Calculus of Deterrence.* Ann Arbor: University of Michigan Press.

Wohlstetter, A. 1959. The Delicate Balance of Terror. *Foreign Affairs* 37: 211-34.

_____. 1974. Is There a Strategic Arms Race? *Foreign Policy* 15:3-20.

Wolfe, T. W. 1970. *Soviet Power and Europe 1945-1970.* Baltimore: Johns Hopkins University Press.

Wolfers, A. 1962. *Discord and Collaboration.* Baltimore: Johns Hopkins University Press.

Wright, M. C. 1957. *The Last Stand of Chinese Conservatism: The Press. T'ung Chih Restoration 1862-1874.* Stanford: Stanford University Press.

Xenophon, trans. Rex Warner. 1949. *The Persian Expedition.* Baltimore: Penguin.

Zartman, I. W., ed. 1978. *Negotiation Process: Theory and Applications.* Beverly Hills: Sage.

Zinnes, D. A. 1968. The Expression and Perception of Hostility in Pre-War Crisis: 1914. In *Quantitative International Politics*, ed. J. D. Singer, pp. 85-119. New York: Free Press.

Manuscript Submission and Previous Publications

MANUSCRIPT SUBMISSION

The *Monograph Series in World Affairs,* published quarterly since 1963 by the Graduate School of International Studies, focuses on theoretic developments and research results dealing with contemporary problems of international relations. In treatment and scope, scholarly pieces that fall between journal and book length manuscripts are suitable. Thoughtful, relevant studies presented analytically in historical and social science frameworks are welcome. Statements of fact or opinion remain the responsibility of the authors alone and do not imply endorsement by the editors or publishers.

Submission: Send manuscripts in triplicate to Karen A. Feste, Editor, Monograph Series in World Affairs, Graduate School of International Studies, University of Denver, Denver, Colorado 80208. Manuscripts already published, scheduled for publication elsewhere, or simultaneously submitted to another journal are not acceptable. Manuscripts will be returned to authors only if accompanied, on submission, by a stamped, self-addressed envelope.

Abstract: Each manuscript must be summarized with a one to two page abstract indicating framework, setting, methodology, and findings.

Author Identification: On a separate page, specify manuscript title, full name and address of author(s), academic or other professional affiliations, and indicate to whom correspondence and galley proofs should be sent. A brief paragraph describing the author's research interest and recent publications should accompany the manuscript. Since manuscripts are sent out anonymously for evaluation, the author's name and affiliation should appear only on a separate covering sheet, as should all footnotes identifying the author.

Form: Manuscripts should be typed double-spaced (including footnotes), with footnotes, references, tables, charts, and figures on separate pages. Authors should follow the Chicago *Manual of Style* except as noted below regarding references. Footnotes should be numbered by chapter. Excessive footnoting should be avoided. Tables, figures, and charts should be mentioned in the text, numbered with Arabic numerals, and given a brief, descriptive title. A guideline should be inserted to indicate their appropriate place in the text.

References: In the text: All source references are to be identified at the appropriate point in the text by the last name of the author, year of publication, and pagination where needed. Identify subsequent citations of the same source in the same way as the first, not using *ibid., op. cit.,* or *loc. sit.* Examples: If author's name is in the text, follow it with year in parentheses [...Morcan, (1969)...]. If author's name is not in the text, insert, in parentheses, the last name and year, separated by a comma [...(Davidson, 1957)...]. Pagination follows year of publication after a colon [...(Budd, 1967:24)...]. Give both last names for dual authors; for more than two, use *et al.* If there is more than one reference to one author and year, distinguish them by letters added to the year [...(1977a)...].

In the Reference Section: The reference section must include all references cited in the text. The use of *et al.* is not acceptable; list the full name of all authors. The format for books: author, year of publication, title, place of publication, publisher. The format for journals: author, year of publication, title of article, name of periodical, volume, number, month, page.

Evaluations: Each manuscript is reviewed by the editor and at least two other readers. Almost always, two reviews are sought outside the University of Denver. General policy is to complete the evaluation process and communicate the editorial decision to the author within four months. Full referee reports are sent to the author. Anonymity of author and reviewer is preserved. Scholars who have furnished reviews of manuscripts during the year will be listed in the final issue of each volume.

Accepted Manuscripts: Manuscripts accepted for publication are subject to copy editing in our office. Edited versions (and later, page proofs) will be sent to the author for approval before materials are given to the printer. These must be returned within ten days. Due to prohibitive cost, substantial changes proposed at the page proof stage will be made at the discretion of the editors; or, alternatively, the cost of such changes will be billed to the author. Instructions for the preparation of camera-ready artwork will be forwarded to the author upon acceptance of the manuscript for publication. This artwork (tables, graphs, figures, photos) must be completed and approved before the production process will be initiated. Ten copies of the published monograph will be supplied free of charge to the senior author.

Permission Policy: To obtain permission to photocopy or to translate materials from the *Monograph Series,* please contact the editor.

Advertising: Current rates and specifications may be obtained by writing the managing editor.

Rates: *Individuals:* single issue, $5.00 plus $1.50 postage and handling; annual subscription, $14.00. *Libraries and Institutions:* annual subscription, $18.00; single issue, $5.00 plus postage and handling. Back issues available at $3.00 per single issue.

Special Offer to Libraries, Institutions, or Individuals

Volumes 1-18 (62 Monographs) — $125.00

— more than a 50% discount —

MONOGRAPH SERIES IN WORLD AFFAIRS

Previous Publications

Volume 1, 1963-1964 Series

Rupert Emerson. *Political Modernization: The Single-Party System.*

Wendell Bell and Ivar Oxall. *Decisions of Nationhood: Political and Social Development in the British Caribbean.*

Volume 2, 1964-1965 Series

John C. Campbell. *The Middle East in the Muted Cold War.*

Dean G. Pruitt. *Problem Solving in the Department of State.*

James R. Scarritt. *Political Change in a Traditional African Clan: A Structural-Functional Analysis of the Nsits of Nigeria.*

Volume 3, 1965-1966 Series

Jack Citrin. *United Nations Peacekeeping Activities: A Case Study in Organizational Task Expansion.*

Ernst B. Haas and Philippe C. Schmitter. *The Politics of Economics in Latin American Regionalism: The Latin American Free Trade Association after Four Years of Operation* (out of print).

Taylor Cole. *The Canadian Bureaucracy and Federalism, 1947-1965.*

Arnold Rivkin. *Africa and the European Common Market: A Perspective.* (Revised Second Edition)

Volume 4, 1966-1967 Series

Edwin C. Hoyt. *National Policy and International Law: Case Studies from American Canal Policy.*

Bruce M. Russett and Carolyn C. Cooper. *Arms Control in Europe: Proposals and Political Constraints.*

Vincent Davis. *The Politics of Innovation: Patterns in Navy Cases.*

Yaroslav Bilinsky. *Changes in the Central Committee Communist Party of the Soviet Union, 1961-1966.*

Volume 5, 1967-1968 Series

Ernst B. Haas. *Collective Security and the Future International System.*

M. Donald Hancock. *Sweden: A Multiparty System in Transition?*

W.A.E. Skurnik, Editor, Rene Lemarchand, Kenneth W. Grundy and Charles F. Andrain. *African Political Thought: Lumumba, Nkrumah, and Toure.*

Volume 6, 1968-1969 Series

Frederick H. Gareau. *The Cold War 1947-1967: A Quantitative Study.*

Henderson B. Braddick. *Germany, Czechoslovakia, and the "Grand Alliance" in the May Crisis, 1938.*

Robert L. Friedheim. *Understanding the Debate on Ocean Resources.*

Richard L. Siegel. *Evaluating the Results of Foreign Policy: Soviet and American Efforts in India.*

Volume 7, 1969-1970 Series

Quincy Wright. *On Predicting International Relations, The Year 2000.*

James N. Rosenau. *Race in International Politics: A Dialogue in Five Parts.*

William S. Tuohy and Barry Ames. *Mexican University Students in Politics: Rebels without Allies?*

Karl H. Hoerning. *Secondary Modernization: Societal Changes of Newly Developing Nations—A Theoretical Essay in Comparative Sociology.*

Volume 8, 1970-1971 Series

Young W. Kihl. *Conflict Issues and International Civil Aviation: Three Cases* (out of print).

Morton Schwartz. *The "Motive Forces" of Soviet Foreign Poicy, A Reappraisal.*

Joseph I. Coffey. *Deterrence in the 1970s* (out of print).

Edward Miles. *International Administration of Space Exploration and Exploitation.*

Volume 9, 1971-1972 Series

Edwin G. Corr. *The Political Process in Colombia.*

Shelton L. Williams. *Nuclear Nonproliferation in International Politics: The Japanese Case.*

Sue Ellen M. Charlton. *The French Left and European Integration.*

Volume 10, 1972-1973 Series

Robert W. Dean. *Nationalism and Political Change in Eastern Europe: The Slovak Question and the Czechoslovak Reform Movement.*

M. Donald Hancock. *The Bundeswehr and the National People's Army: A Comparative Study of German Civil-Military Polity.*

Louis Rene Beres. *The Management of World Power: A Theoretical Analysis.*

George A. Kourvetaris and Betty A. Dobratz. *Social Origins and Political Orientations of Officer Corps in a World Perspective.*

Volume 11, 1973-1974 Series

Waltraud Q. Morales. *Social Revolution: Theory and Historical Application.*

David O'Shea. *Education, the Social System, and Development.*

Robert H. Bates. *Patterns of Uneven Development: Causes and Consequences in Zambia.*

Robert L. Peterson. *Career Motivations of Administrators and Their Impact in the European Community.*

Volume 12, 1974-1975 Series

Craig Liske and Barry Rundquist. *The Politics of Weapons Procurement: The Role of Congress.*

Barry M. Schutz and Douglas Scott. *Natives and Settlers: A Comparative Analysis of the Politics of Opposition and Mobilization in Northern Ireland and Rhodesia.*

Vincent B. Khapoya. *The Politics of Decision: A Comparative Study of African Policy Toward the Liberation Movements.*

Louis Rene Beres. *Transforming World Politics: The National Roots of World Peace.*

Volume 13, 1975-1976 Series

Wayne S. Vucinich. *A Study in Social Survival: Katun in the Bileca Rudine.*

Jan F. Triska and Paul M. Johnson. *Political Development and Political Change in Eastern Europe: A Comparative Study.*

Louis L. Ortmayer. *Conflict, Compromise, and Conciliation: West German-Polish Normalization 1966-1976.*

James B. Bruce. *Politics of Soviet Policy Formation: Khrushchev's Innovative Policies in Education and Agriculture.*

Volume 14, 1976-1977 Series

Daniel J. O'Neil. *Three Perennial Themes of Anti-Colonialism: The Irish Case.*

Thomas Lobe. *United States National Security Policy and Aid to the Thailand Police.*

David F. Cusack. *Revolution and Reaction: The Internal and International Dynamics of Conflict and Confrontation in Chile.*

David F. Cusack. *The Death of Democracy and Revolution in Chile, 1970-1973.* Slide Show-Narrative Cassette (out of print).

Robert E. Harkavy. *Spectre of a Middle Eastern Holocaust: The Strategic and Diplomatic Implications of the Israeli Nuclear Weapons Program.*

Volume 15, 1977-1978 Series

Lewis W. Snider. *Arabesque: Untangling the Patterns of Conventional Arms Supply to Israel and the Arab States and the Implications for United States Policy on Supply of "Lethal" Weapons to Egypt.*

Bennett Ramberg. *The Seabed Arms Control Negotiations: A Study of Multilateral Arms Control Conference Diplomacy.*

Todd M. Sandler, William Loehr, and Jon T. Cauley. *The Political Economy of Public Goods and International Cooperation.*

Ronald M. Grant and E. Spencer Wellhofer, Editors. *Ethno-Nationalism, Multinational Corporations, and the Modern State.*

Volume 16, 1978-1979 Series

Sophia Peterson. *Sino-Soviet-American Relations: Conflict, Communication and Mutual Threat.*

Robert H. Donaldson. *The Soviet-Indian Alignment: Quest for Influence.*

Volume 17, 1979-1980 Series

Pat McGowan and Helen E. Purkitt. *Demystifying "National Character" in Black Africa: A Comparative Study of Culture and Foreign Policy Behavior.*

Theodore H. Cohn. *Canadian Food Aid: Domestic and Foreign Policy Implications.*

Robert A. Hoover. *Arms Control: The Interwar Naval Limitation Agreements.*

Lisa Robock Shaffer and Stephen M. Shaffer. *The Politics of International Cooperation: A Comparison of U.S. Experience in Space and in Security.*

Volume 18, 1980-1981 Series

Massiye Edwin Koloko. *The Manpower Approach to Planning: Theoretical Issues and Evidence from Zambia.*

Harry Eckstein. *The Natural History of Congruence Theory.*

P. Terrence Hopmann, Dina A. Zinnes, and J. David Singer. *Cumulation in International Relations Research.*

Philip A. Schrodt. *Preserving Arms Distributions in a Multi-Polar World: A Mathematical Study.*

Volume 19, 1981-1982 Series

Michael D. Ward. *Research Gaps in Alliance Dynamics.*

Theresa C. Smith. *Trojan Peace: Some Deterrence Propositions Tested.*

In 1982 as in every year since 1954

AFRICA TODAY

is in the vanguard
of analysis and interpretation
of African affairs.

". . . must be on the reading list of every concerned Africanist scholar."
David Wiley, Michigan State University

". . . high standards of scholarship . . . diversity of concern . . .
usefulness to specialists and laymen . . ."

Victor T. LeVine, Washington University
". . . in the vanguard of analysis and awareness."
Timothy M. Shaw, Dalhousie University

George W. Shepherd, Jr., Tilden J. LeMelle, editors

Edward A. Hawley, executive editor

80 or more pages in each quarterly issue

articles, book reviews, new publications

SUBSCRIPTION RATES

		Individuals	Institutions
North &	1 yr.	$12.00	$18.00
South America	2 yr.	$22.00	$33.00
	3 yr.	$31.00	$45.00
	Student (1 yr.)	$9.00	

Elsewhere   **Add $2.00 per year for surface mail.**
Add $8.00 per year for air mail.

AFRICA TODAY

c/o Graduate School of
International Studies
University of Denver
Denver, Colorado 80208

THE FLETCHER FORUM

putting the pieces in place

Published in January and May each year, *The Fletcher Forum*
features articles on diplomacy, international law, politics
and economics, as well as shorter commentaries and book reviews.

☐ $9 One year — two issues
(Foreign subscription) $13

☐ $17 Two years — four issues
(Foreign subscription $24)

☐ $24 Three years — six issues
(Foreign subscription $36)

☐ $15 Institutions — one year
(Foreign institutions $20)

Send your payment to: The Fletcher School of Law
and Diplomacy
Tufts University
Medford, Massachusetts 02155

THE FLETCHER FORUM

INTERNATIONAL STUDIES NOTES
of the International Studies Association

— a forum for conflicting views —

INTERNATIONAL STUDIES NOTES is published to provide a challenging *multidisciplinary* forum for exchange of research, curricular and program reports on international affairs. It is designed to serve teachers, scholars, practitioners, and others concerned with the international arena.

Recent and future topics include: terror; science, technology and development; classroom simulations; human rights; local-global links; gaps between policymakers and academics; contradictory approaches to international affairs; summaries/comments on professional meetings.

Recent contributors have included Norman D. Palmer, David P. Forsythe, James N. Roseneau, Robert C. North, and Rose Hayden.

— RECOMMEND A SUBSCRIPTION TO YOUR LIBRARIAN —

INTERNATIONAL STUDIES NOTES of the International Studies Association is published quarterly by the University of Nebraska-Lincoln and the University of Wyoming and is edited by Joan Wadlow and Leslie Duly.

Subscription Rates: One year $20.00; two years $36.00.

Send subscriptions to: Leslie Duly, 1223 Oldfather Hall, University of Nebraska-Lincoln, Lincoln, Nebraska 68588.

Book format and printing
by
DEPARTMENT OF GRAPHICS
University of Denver